1

The Rise and Fall of Artificial Intelligence

Brandon Taul

Contents

Chapter 1: Genesis of a Dream

In this chapter, we explore the early history and the foundational ideas that sparked the birth of artificial intelligence. From the groundbreaking work of Alan Turing to the Dartmouth Conference in 1956, we witness the inception of AI as a promising new field of study.

In the early 20th century, as humanity stood on the cusp of technological progress, visionaries like Alan Turing began to dream of creating machines that could mimic human intelligence. Alan Turing, a British mathematician, and computer scientist, laid the groundwork for modern artificial intelligence in 1936 with his concept of a universal computing machine, now famously known as the "Turing machine." This theoretical model demonstrated that any computation could be executed through a series of well-defined steps, marking the birth of the digital computer. The idea of creating machines that could think and reason like humans continued to evolve over the years. However, it wasn't until the summer of 1956 when the field of artificial intelligence officially came into being. The Dartmouth Conference, organized by John McCarthy, Marvin Minsky, Nathaniel Rochester, and Claude Shannon, brought together prominent researchers and pioneers in the emerging field. During the conference, McCarthy proposed the term "artificial intelligence" to describe the goal of creating machines capable of intelligent behavior.

Inspired by the prospect of developing intelligent machines, the attendees of the Dartmouth Conference set forth a vision to create programs that could perform tasks previously thought to require human intelligence. They believed that by programming computers to follow rules, they could simulate human decision-making processes and even replicate human thought.

Early AI research primarily focused on symbolic AI, also known as "good old-fashioned AI" (GOFAI). Researchers attempted to encode human knowledge and reasoning into computer programs using symbolic representations and logical rules. The hope was that these systems could understand language, solve complex problems, and exhibit human-like cognition.

Throughout the 1960s and 1970s, AI research made significant strides in problem-solving and game-playing. Programs like the General Problem Solver (GPS) and the Logic Theorist showed promise in tackling logic puzzles and mathematical theorems. These successes fueled enthusiasm and optimism about the future of AI, leading to increased funding and support from both the government and private sectors.

However, as researchers delved deeper into the complexities of human cognition, they realized that replicating human intelligence was far more challenging than they initially anticipated. The limitations of early AI systems, coupled with a lack of computing power, led to an "AI winter" in the late 1970s and early 1980s. Funding for AI research dwindled, and many believed that the dream of creating true artificial intelligence was nothing more than science fiction. Despite these setbacks, some researchers persisted, advocating for a different approach to AI. The field of machine learning emerged as an alternative paradigm, emphasizing the ability of machines to learn from data and adapt their behavior without explicit programming. This marked a turning point in AI research and paved the way for the next era of AI development.

The History

The history of artificial intelligence is a fascinating journey that spans several decades and has witnessed remarkable achievements, setbacks, and paradigm shifts. Let's delve deeper into the key milestones and developments in the history of AI:

Early Concepts and Foundations (1940s-1950s): The groundwork for AI was laid in the early 20th century with theoretical concepts like Alan Turing's "Turing machine" and the notion of universal computing. These ideas provided a theoretical framework for computation and the idea that any computable problem could be solved algorithmically.

The Dartmouth Conference (1956): The Dartmouth Conference, held in the summer of 1956, is often considered the official birth of artificial intelligence as a field of study. At this conference, the term "artificial intelligence" was coined, and researchers set forth the goal of creating machines that could demonstrate intelligent behavior.

Symbolic AI and Early Research (1950s-1960s): In the early years of AI research, the focus was on symbolic AI, where researchers attempted to represent human knowledge and reasoning using symbols and logical rules. Early AI programs, such as the Logic Theorist and the General Problem Solver, showed promise in solving logic puzzles and performing certain problem-solving tasks.

The AI Winter (1970s-1980s): The field of AI faced significant challenges and setbacks during the 1970s and 1980s, often referred to as the "AI winter." Progress was slow, and the initial optimism surrounding AI gave way to skepticism and reduced funding. Many believed that AI was overhyped and that achieving human-like intelligence was far beyond the reach of existing technology.

Expert Systems and Knowledge-Based AI (1970s-1980s): During the AI winter, researchers focused on expert systems, which were rule-based programs designed to mimic the expertise of human specialists in specific domains. Expert systems demonstrated practical applications and found success in areas like medical diagnosis and finance.

The Renaissance of AI: Machine Learning (1980s-1990s): The AI field experienced a resurgence in the 1980s and 1990s with the emergence of machine learning as a key approach. Machine learning shifted the focus from explicitly programmed rules to algorithms that could learn from data and improve their performance over time. Neural networks, genetic algorithms, and other machine learning techniques gained prominence.

AI in the Digital Age (2000s-2010s): Advancements in computing power, data availability, and algorithmic improvements propelled AI to new heights. Applications of AI proliferated in various domains, including natural language processing, image recognition, robotics, and autonomous vehicles. Companies like Google, Amazon, and Apple heavily invested in AI technologies, leading to widespread adoption and integration into everyday life.

Deep Learning and AI Breakthroughs (2010s): Deep learning, a subset of machine learning based on neural networks with multiple layers, became a game-changer in AI research. Breakthroughs in deep learning enabled significant advancements in speech recognition, image analysis, and other AI applications. Projects like AlphaGo demonstrated the ability of AI to outperform human experts in complex games like Go.

Ethical Challenges and AI Governance: The rapid expansion of AI raised ethical concerns regarding data privacy, bias, job displacement, and the impact of AI on society. Governments and organizations worldwide started addressing the need for AI governance, regulations, and ethical frameworks to ensure responsible AI development and deployment.

The Future of AI: Researchers and innovators are working on developing explainable AI, AI safety, and human-AI collaboration. The quest for artificial general intelligence (AGI), an AI system capable of understanding and learning any intellectual task that a human can, remains a long-term ambition.

The history of artificial intelligence is an ongoing story, with new chapters being written every day. As AI continues to shape our world, the journey remains filled with excitement, challenges, and boundless possibilities.

The Foundation

The foundation of artificial intelligence (AI) can be traced back to several key concepts and foundational ideas that set the stage for the development of this fascinating field. Let's delve deeper into the key elements that form the bedrock of AI:

Turing Machine and Computability (1936): In 1936, British mathematician and computer scientist Alan Turing introduced the concept of a theoretical computational device called the Turing machine. This abstract machine could simulate any computation through a series of well-defined steps, using a tape with symbols and a head that could read and write those symbols. Turing's work laid the foundation for the theory of computation and provided a formal basis for understanding the limits of computability and the notion of algorithms.

Logic and Symbolic Reasoning: Early AI researchers were inspired by the idea that human intelligence could be emulated through symbolic reasoning. The goal was to represent knowledge and reasoning in a formal, logical language that could be processed by machines. This approach, known as symbolic AI or GOFAI (Good Old-Fashioned AI), involved encoding human expertise and decision-making as rules and logical statements.

The Dartmouth Conference (1956): In the summer of 1956, a group of researchers organized the Dartmouth Conference, which is considered the birth of AI as a field of study. During this conference, the term "artificial intelligence" was coined, and the attendees laid out a vision for creating machines that could exhibit intelligent behavior.

Early AI Programs: In the late 1950s and 1960s, AI researchers developed early AI programs to demonstrate machine intelligence. Notable examples include:

The Logic Theorist: Developed by Allen Newell and Herbert A. Simon, this program used heuristic search to prove mathematical theorems in symbolic logic.
The General Problem Solver (GPS): Also by Newell and Simon, GPS was one of the first AI programs designed to solve general problems by searching through possible solutions.
AI Winter and Expert Systems: Despite initial enthusiasm, AI research faced significant challenges in the 1970s and early 1980s, leading to what was known as the "AI winter."

Progress was slow, and funding declined. However, during this period, researchers turned their attention to expert systems, which were rule-based programs that attempted to replicate the expertise of human specialists in specific domains. Expert systems demonstrated practical applications and found success in areas like medical diagnosis and finance.

Machine Learning and Neural Networks: In the 1980s and 1990s, AI experienced a resurgence with the emergence of machine learning as a key approach. Machine learning shifted the focus from explicit programming to algorithms that could learn from data. Neural networks, inspired by the structure of the human brain, gained popularity as a machine learning technique.

The Digital Age and Big Data: The 2000s saw a significant expansion of AI due to advancements in computing power and the availability of vast amounts of data. Big data became a critical driver for machine learning algorithms to extract patterns and insights from large datasets.

Deep Learning: The breakthrough in deep learning, especially around the late 2000s and early 2010s, revolutionized AI. Deep learning, a subset of machine learning based on neural networks with multiple layers, showed unprecedented success in tasks like image recognition, natural language processing, and game playing.

These foundational ideas and developments paved the way for the AI we see today. AI continues to evolve, with new breakthroughs in areas like reinforcement learning, unsupervised learning, and ethical considerations surrounding AI applications. The foundation of AI will continue to influence the field's future growth and potential societal impact.

Chapter 1 of "The Rise and Fall of Artificial Intelligence" traces the roots of AI back to its inception and explores the early motivations and challenges faced by pioneers in the field. It sets the stage for the subsequent chapters, delving into the golden age of AI, the revolutionary breakthroughs, and the transformative impact of artificial intelligence on society. The journey of AI has been one of fascination, hope, and continuous innovation, but the road ahead is full of uncertainties and ethical dilemmas that demand our attention and thoughtful consideration.

Chapter 2: The Golden Age

The Golden Age of AI showcases the rapid advancements in the 1980s and 1990s, driven by the development of expert systems and machine learning algorithms. We delve into the optimism surrounding AI's potential to revolutionize industries and transform the world.

The Golden Age of AI was a period of tremendous progress and excitement for the field, characterized by significant advancements in both research and application of artificial intelligence. Spanning from the late 1980s to the early 2000s, this era witnessed breakthroughs that laid the groundwork for the AI revolution that followed. In this chapter, we explore the key developments and milestones that defined the Golden Age of AI.

Expert Systems and Commercialization: During the Golden Age, expert systems saw widespread adoption in various industries. These rule-based systems, which emulated the decision-making processes of human experts in specific domains, found practical applications in fields such as finance, healthcare, and manufacturing. Expert systems were commercialized, leading to the rise of AI startups and companies offering AI solutions to businesses.

Natural Language Processing (NLP) and Speech Recognition: Advancements in NLP and speech recognition played a pivotal role in making AI more accessible and user-friendly. Researchers made strides in developing algorithms that could understand and generate human language, enabling technologies like speech-to-text, text-to-speech, and machine translation.

Chess and Game Playing: In 1997, a historic moment in AI history occurred when IBM's Deep Blue defeated world chess champion Garry Kasparov in a six-game match. This victory showcased the power of AI in strategic decision-making and propelled interest in AI applications in game playing.

Robotics and Autonomous Systems: The Golden Age saw significant developments in robotics and autonomous systems. AI-powered robots and drones began to perform complex tasks in manufacturing, logistics, and exploration. Autonomous vehicles also became a focus of research, with various experiments and competitions showcasing the potential for self-driving cars.

Machine Learning Renaissance: Machine learning experienced a resurgence during the Golden Age, fueled by the availability of large datasets and increased computational power. Researchers explored new machine learning algorithms, including support vector machines, random forests, and ensemble methods. These techniques demonstrated remarkable success in pattern recognition, classification, and regression tasks.

AI in Medicine and Healthcare: AI's potential to revolutionize healthcare was recognized during the Golden Age. AI algorithms were applied to medical diagnosis, drug discovery, and personalized treatment recommendations. Expert systems and machine learning models assisted doctors in interpreting medical images and identifying potential diseases.

Emergence of AI Research Centers: Prominent AI research centers, such as the Stanford AI Lab, MIT Computer Science and Artificial Intelligence Laboratory (CSAIL), and the University of California, Berkeley's Artificial Intelligence Research Lab (BAIR), played a crucial role in fostering innovation and collaboration among AI researchers.

Limitations and Challenges: Despite the significant progress, AI systems still faced limitations and challenges during the Golden Age. Expert systems struggled with handling uncertainty and lacked adaptability. Machine learning algorithms were often data-hungry and prone to overfitting. Moreover, the "AI winter" left some skepticism in the academic and industrial communities regarding the long-term viability of AI technologies.

The Golden Age of AI laid the foundation for the subsequent AI revolution. The advancements made during this era provided crucial insights into the capabilities and limitations of AI systems, setting the stage for the transformative impact AI would have on various industries and aspects of our daily lives. As AI entered the 21st century, its potential was set to soar, ushering in a new era of innovation and societal change.

Rapid Advancements in AI:

The rapid advancements of AI have been a hallmark of its recent history, particularly in the last decade or so. These advancements have been driven by a combination of factors, including increased computational power, the availability of massive amounts of data, breakthroughs in algorithms, and the growing interest and investment from both academia and industry. Let's explore some key areas where AI has seen rapid progress:

Deep Learning and Neural Networks: Deep learning, a subset of machine learning based on neural networks with multiple layers, has been a game-changer in AI research. Breakthroughs in training deep neural networks, such as convolutional neural networks (CNNs) for image recognition and recurrent neural networks (RNNs) for natural language processing, have significantly improved the performance of AI systems. The availability of large-scale labeled datasets, like

ImageNet and OpenAI's GPT, has fueled the success of deep learning models.

Natural Language Processing (NLP) and Language Models: NLP has made remarkable progress, enabling machines to understand and generate human language more effectively. Pre-trained language models, such as OpenAI's GPT-3, have demonstrated the ability to perform a wide range of language tasks, from text completion and translation to question-answering and chatbot interactions. These models leverage vast amounts of data and transfer learning to achieve impressive language understanding.

Computer Vision and Image Recognition: Advancements in computer vision have led to breakthroughs in image recognition and object detection. AI systems can now identify and classify objects in images and videos with high accuracy, enabling applications in autonomous vehicles, surveillance, medical imaging, and more.

Reinforcement Learning and Game Playing: Reinforcement learning, a branch of machine learning focused on decision-making in dynamic environments, has achieved significant milestones in game playing. AI agents have beaten human champions in complex games like Go, chess, and Dota 2, showcasing the power of AI to master strategic decision-making.

AI in Healthcare and Medicine: AI is making rapid strides in healthcare and medicine. AI-powered systems are being used for medical image analysis, disease diagnosis, drug discovery, and personalized treatment recommendations. These applications have the potential to improve patient outcomes and streamline healthcare processes.

Autonomous Systems: AI is playing a pivotal role in the development of autonomous systems, such as self-driving cars and drones. Significant progress has been made in creating AI algorithms that can perceive and navigate real-world environments, bringing autonomous vehicles closer to widespread adoption.

Robotics and Automation: AI-driven robots are becoming more sophisticated and capable of performing a wide range of tasks. From manufacturing and logistics to elderly care and disaster response, AI-powered robots are being deployed in diverse scenarios to augment human capabilities.

Ethical AI and AI Safety: As AI technologies advance, the focus on ethical AI and AI safety has intensified. Researchers and policymakers are actively working on developing guidelines and regulations to ensure that AI is developed and deployed responsibly, avoiding potential biases and harmful consequences.

Integration into Various Industries: AI is rapidly permeating various industries, including finance, marketing, entertainment, and agriculture. Companies are leveraging AI to enhance customer experiences, optimize processes, and make data-driven decisions.

The rapid advancements in AI have ushered in a new era of innovation, transforming the way we interact with technology and the world around us. However, with these advancements come new challenges related to ethics, privacy, security, and the potential impact on jobs and society. Addressing these challenges will be essential as AI continues to evolve and play an increasingly significant role in our lives.

Expert Systems and Machine Learning Algorithms

Expert Systems:

Expert Systems are a type of artificial intelligence that emulates the decision-making ability of human experts in specific domains. They are rule-based systems that use a knowledge base, which contains a set of rules and facts, and an inference engine, which applies the rules to the facts to make decisions or solve problems.

Components of Expert Systems:

Knowledge Base: The knowledge base contains a collection of rules and facts relevant to a specific domain. These rules are typically represented in the form of "if-then" statements, where the "if" part describes the conditions or inputs, and the "then" part describes the actions or outputs.

Inference Engine: The inference engine is responsible for applying the rules from the knowledge base to the given facts or inputs. It uses logical reasoning and deduction to arrive at conclusions or solutions.

Advantages of Expert Systems:

Domain Expertise: Expert Systems can capture and retain the knowledge of domain experts, making it accessible to a broader audience.

Consistency: Expert Systems provide consistent decision-making and problem-solving, as they follow predefined rules and logic.

Explanation: Expert Systems can explain their reasoning, making them more transparent and understandable to users.

Limitations of Expert Systems:

Domain Specificity: Expert Systems are limited to the specific domain for which they are designed. They lack the ability to generalize knowledge across different domains.

Knowledge Acquisition: Constructing the knowledge base can be time-consuming and requires the expertise of human domain experts.

Uncertainty Handling: Expert Systems struggle to handle uncertainty and ambiguity, which are prevalent in real-world situations.

Machine Learning Algorithms: Machine Learning (ML) is a subset of artificial intelligence that focuses on the development of algorithms that can learn from data and improve their performance over time without being explicitly programmed. Machine learning algorithms can recognize patterns, make predictions, and adapt to new information.

Types of Machine Learning Algorithms:

a. Supervised Learning: In supervised learning, the algorithm is trained on a labeled dataset, where each data point is associated with a corresponding label or output. The algorithm learns to map inputs to outputs by minimizing the difference between predicted and actual labels. Examples include classification and regression tasks.

b. Unsupervised Learning: In unsupervised learning, the algorithm is given an unlabeled dataset and seeks to find patterns or structures within the data without any predefined output. Clustering and dimensionality reduction are common examples of unsupervised learning tasks.

c. Reinforcement Learning: Reinforcement learning involves an agent that interacts with an environment to achieve a goal. The agent receives feedback in the form of rewards or penalties, allowing it to learn from its actions and improve decision-making over time.

Advantages of Machine Learning Algorithms:

Data-Driven Decision Making: Machine learning algorithms can extract insights and patterns from vast amounts of data, enabling data-driven decision-making in various domains. Adaptability: Machine learning algorithms can adapt and improve their performance as new data becomes available, making them suitable for dynamic and evolving environments. Generalization: Machine learning algorithms can generalize patterns learned from training data to make predictions on unseen data.

Limitations of Machine Learning Algorithms:

Data Requirements: Machine learning algorithms often require large amounts of high-quality data for effective training, which may not always be readily available.
Overfitting: There is a risk of overfitting, where a model performs well on the training data but poorly on unseen data, if the model is too complex or the training data is not representative.
Interpretability: Some complex machine learning models, such as deep neural networks, lack interpretability, making it challenging to understand their decision-making process.

Both Expert Systems and Machine Learning Algorithms have their strengths and weaknesses, and they are often used in combination to complement each other's capabilities in various AI applications. Expert Systems excel in well-defined domains with explicit rules and knowledge, while Machine Learning Algorithms thrive in data-rich environments with complex patterns and relationships.

Chapter 3: The AI Revolution

This chapter explores the transformative impact of AI on various sectors, including healthcare, finance, transportation, and entertainment. AI's growing presence in society leads to profound societal changes, both positive and negative.

The AI Revolution marks a pivotal moment in history when artificial intelligence transcended its earlier limitations and began to permeate almost every aspect of human life. Spanning from the late 20th century to the present day, this chapter explores the transformative impact of AI across various sectors and the profound changes it brought to society.

AI in Healthcare: The AI Revolution revolutionized healthcare by enhancing diagnosis, treatment, and patient care. AI-powered medical imaging systems improved the accuracy and speed of disease detection, enabling early diagnosis of conditions like cancer and neurological disorders. Virtual health assistants and chatbots provided personalized health advice and support, especially in remote or underserved areas. Additionally, AI-driven drug discovery expedited the identification of potential compounds for new medications.

Financial Services and AI: AI's application in the financial industry led to significant improvements in risk assessment, fraud detection, and investment strategies. Machine learning algorithms analyzed vast amounts of financial data to make better predictions about market trends and customer behavior. Robo-advisors emerged, offering automated investment advice based on individual financial goals and risk tolerance.

AI and Transportation: The AI Revolution had a profound impact on transportation, with AI playing a critical role in the development of autonomous vehicles. Self-driving cars and trucks promised safer and more efficient transportation, reducing accidents caused by human error and optimizing traffic flow. AI-driven navigation apps transformed the way people plan their routes and avoid congested areas.

AI and Education: The integration of AI in education led to personalized learning experiences for students. Adaptive learning platforms assessed individual students' strengths and weaknesses, tailoring educational content and pacing to optimize learning outcomes. Virtual tutors and AI-powered language learning applications offered personalized coaching and feedback to learners.

Entertainment and Content Creation: AI significantly impacted the entertainment industry, from movie recommendations on streaming platforms to AI-generated music and art. Recommendation algorithms analyzed user preferences to curate personalized content recommendations, enriching user experiences. AI-generated content, including music compositions and visual art, showcased the creative potential of AI systems.

AI in Customer Service: The AI Revolution brought chatbots and virtual assistants to the forefront of customer service. Companies used AI-powered chatbots to engage with customers, provide support, and resolve queries efficiently. Natural Language Processing (NLP) and sentiment analysis algorithms enabled chatbots to understand and respond to customer inquiries more effectively.

AI and Environmental Sustainability: AI contributed to environmental sustainability efforts by optimizing energy consumption and improving resource management. Smart grids used AI algorithms to balance energy supply and demand, reducing waste and carbon emissions. AI-driven precision agriculture improved crop yields by monitoring and optimizing irrigation, fertilization, and pest control.

Ethical Considerations: The AI Revolution also brought ethical considerations to the forefront. As AI systems gained more autonomy and influence, questions arose about AI ethics, accountability, and bias. Researchers, policymakers, and industry stakeholders grappled with the challenge of developing responsible AI frameworks to ensure fairness, transparency, and safety in AI applications.

AI and Employment: The widespread adoption of AI led to both opportunities and concerns regarding employment. While AI automation improved efficiency and productivity in many industries, it also raised concerns about job displacement. The need for reskilling and upskilling the workforce became evident to adapt to the changing demands of the AI-driven job market.

AI and Privacy: As AI systems processed vast amounts of data, privacy and data protection became pressing concerns. Striking a balance between AI's data-driven capabilities and individual privacy rights became a challenge for policymakers and organizations. AI applications in surveillance and data profiling further amplified the need for robust privacy regulations.

The AI Revolution continues to unfold, with new breakthroughs, challenges, and ethical considerations arising regularly. As AI technology evolves, society must navigate the opportunities and complexities it presents while ensuring that AI serves the greater good and contributes positively to humanity's progress.

Transformative impact of AI

The transformative impact of AI (Artificial Intelligence) has been profound, reshaping various aspects of human life and industries across the globe. Below are some key areas where AI has had a transformative effect:

Enhanced Efficiency and Productivity: AI has revolutionized industries by automating repetitive tasks and optimizing processes. AI-driven automation has led to increased efficiency, reduced operational costs, and faster decision-making. In manufacturing, for instance, AI-powered robots have improved production speed and accuracy, leading to higher output and reduced errors.

Personalization and Customization: AI's ability to analyze vast amounts of data has enabled personalized experiences for users. Online retailers and streaming platforms use AI algorithms to recommend products, movies, and music based on individual preferences and behaviors. This personalized approach enhances user satisfaction and engagement.

Improved Healthcare and Medical Diagnostics: AI has significantly impacted the healthcare sector by improving medical diagnostics and treatment plans. AI-powered medical imaging systems can detect diseases with greater accuracy and speed, leading to early diagnosis and better patient outcomes. Additionally, AI assists healthcare providers in identifying optimal treatment strategies based on patient data.

Revolutionizing Education: AI is transforming education through personalized learning experiences and smart tutoring systems. Adaptive learning platforms use AI algorithms to analyze student progress and tailor educational content accordingly, optimizing learning outcomes. AI-based virtual tutors offer personalized feedback and guidance to learners.

Autonomous Vehicles and Transportation: AI's breakthrough in autonomous vehicles is revolutionizing transportation. Self-driving cars and trucks promise safer, more efficient transportation while reducing accidents caused by human error.

Additionally, AI-powered navigation systems optimize travel routes, easing congestion and reducing travel time.

AI in Finance and Banking: AI has revolutionized the financial industry, streamlining operations, and improving customer experiences. Machine learning algorithms assess financial data to make better predictions about market trends and customer behavior. Robo-advisors offer personalized investment advice, while AI-powered fraud detection systems protect against financial crimes.

Advanced Natural Language Processing: Natural Language Processing (NLP) has empowered AI systems to comprehend and generate human language effectively. Virtual assistants like Siri and Alexa can answer questions, perform tasks, and interact conversationally with users. NLP has also transformed customer service through AI-powered chatbots that resolve queries efficiently.

Environmental Sustainability: AI is being employed to address environmental challenges and promote sustainability. Smart grids use AI algorithms to optimize energy distribution, reducing waste and carbon emissions. AI-driven precision agriculture optimizes resource usage and enhances crop yields while minimizing environmental impact.

AI in Creative Industries: AI is making its mark in creative fields, including music composition, art, and content creation. AI-generated music compositions and art pieces have sparked interest and debates about the intersection of human creativity and AI capabilities.

AI for Social Good: AI is being utilized for social good and humanitarian efforts. AI algorithms aid disaster response by analyzing data to predict and mitigate potential disasters. AI-powered systems also assist in monitoring endangered species and protecting the environment.

While AI has unlocked numerous opportunities and benefits, it also raises concerns regarding privacy, ethical considerations, job displacement, and the potential for biased decision-making. As AI continues to evolve, it is crucial to strike a balance between its transformative potential and responsible use to ensure that it serves humanity's best interests and promotes a sustainable and inclusive future.

AI's Growing Presence in Society

AI's growing presence in society has been a defining characteristic of the modern era, impacting various aspects of daily life, business, governance, and culture. Below are key areas where AI has become increasingly prevalent:

Everyday Technology and Gadgets: AI is integrated into many devices and gadgets used in everyday life. Smartphones, smart speakers, and virtual assistants like Siri, Alexa, and Google Assistant leverage AI to understand voice commands and provide personalized responses. AI-powered applications, such as predictive text messaging and personalized news feeds, have become common.

E-Commerce and Retail: AI has revolutionized e-commerce and retail by providing personalized shopping experiences. AI-driven recommendation engines suggest products based on individual preferences and browsing behavior, improving customer engagement and increasing sales. AI-powered chatbots provide instant customer support and assistance.

Social Media and Content Curation: AI algorithms play a significant role in social media platforms, curating personalized content feeds and targeting advertisements to users based on their interests and behaviors. AI-driven content moderation tools help identify and remove harmful content, ensuring a safer online environment.

Healthcare and Medical Diagnostics: AI's presence in healthcare is expanding rapidly. AI-powered medical imaging systems aid in the early detection of diseases like cancer, enabling more accurate diagnoses. AI algorithms analyze patient data to suggest treatment plans, optimize drug dosages, and predict health outcomes.

Finance and Banking: AI is transforming the financial sector by automating processes, detecting fraudulent activities, and making data-driven investment decisions. AI-driven chatbots and virtual assistants assist customers with banking services, inquiries, and support.

Transportation and Autonomous Systems: AI is a driving force behind the development of autonomous vehicles, improving road safety and transportation efficiency. AI-powered traffic management systems optimize traffic flow, reducing congestion and travel time. Additionally, ride-sharing services use AI algorithms to match drivers and riders efficiently.

Entertainment and Content Creation: AI is contributing to the creation and curation of entertainment content. AI-generated music compositions, art, and even screenplays are gaining attention. Content platforms use AI to personalize recommendations for users, improving user engagement and content consumption.

Cybersecurity and Data Protection: AI is employed in cybersecurity to detect and prevent cyber threats. AI algorithms analyze network traffic patterns to identify potential security breaches and mitigate cyberattacks. AI also helps protect user data by detecting anomalies and unauthorized access.

Smart Homes and Internet of Things (IoT): AI plays a crucial role in creating smart homes, where various devices and appliances are connected and controlled through AI-powered systems. Smart thermostats, lighting, and security systems adjust to user preferences and routines, enhancing convenience and energy efficiency.

Governance and Public Services: AI is being adopted by governments to enhance public services. AI-driven chatbots assist citizens with inquiries and government processes. AI is also used for data analysis to inform policy decisions and improve urban planning.

As AI's presence in society continues to grow, it brings with it various opportunities and challenges. While AI offers the potential to improve efficiency, convenience, and decision-making, it also raises concerns about privacy, bias, job displacement, and ethical considerations. Striking a balance between the benefits and challenges is essential to ensure that AI's integration into society promotes the well-being of individuals and the collective good.

Chapter 4: Ethical Dilemmas

As AI becomes increasingly integrated into our lives, it raises a host of ethical questions. We discuss the challenges of ensuring fairness, transparency, and accountability in AI systems. Topics include bias, privacy concerns, and the dilemmas faced by policymakers.

Artificial intelligence continues to proliferate and shape various aspects of our lives, it presents a myriad of ethical dilemmas that demand thoughtful consideration and responsible decision-making. This chapter explores some of the key ethical challenges arising from AI's rapid advancement:

Privacy and Data Protection: AI systems often rely on vast amounts of data to function effectively. The collection, storage, and use of personal data raise concerns about privacy and data protection. As AI applications become more pervasive, safeguarding individual data and ensuring transparency in data usage become crucial ethical considerations.

Bias and Fairness: AI algorithms are susceptible to bias, reflecting the biases present in the data they are trained on. Biased AI systems can perpetuate discrimination and inequality, affecting decisions related to hiring, lending, and criminal justice. Ensuring fairness in AI decision-making and mitigating bias require careful attention and diverse representation in the development process.

Autonomy and Accountability: As AI systems become more autonomous, they make decisions that have significant impacts on individuals and society. The question of who should be held accountable for AI decisions and actions becomes complex.

Ensuring a clear chain of responsibility and defining legal frameworks for AI accountability are crucial ethical challenges. Job Displacement and Workforce Transition: The widespread adoption of AI automation raises concerns about job displacement and workforce transition. While AI can create new job opportunities, it can also render certain job roles obsolete. Ensuring a smooth transition for affected workers through reskilling and upskilling programs is an ethical imperative.

Autonomous Weapons and Lethal AI: The development of autonomous weapons raises ethical dilemmas about the use of lethal AI in military contexts. The lack of human control in decision-making can lead to unintended consequences and raise moral questions about the use of AI in warfare.

Algorithmic Transparency and Explainability: As AI systems become more complex, their decision-making processes can become inscrutable, leading to the "black box" problem. Ensuring algorithmic transparency and explainability is crucial, particularly in critical applications like healthcare and justice systems, where the reasons behind AI decisions have significant implications.

Impact on Mental Health and Well-being: AI applications, especially in social media and content curation, can impact users' mental health and well-being. Personalized content feeds can lead to echo chambers and contribute to misinformation or extremist views. Striking a balance between personalization and promoting diverse perspectives becomes an ethical challenge.

Exploitative AI and User Manipulation: AI can be utilized to manipulate user behavior for commercial gain or political influence. The ethical question of user manipulation, particularly in the context of social media and advertising, demands attention to ensure AI is used responsibly and respects user autonomy.

Ownership of AI-Generated Content: AI-generated content, such as art, music, and literature, raises questions about intellectual property and authorship. Defining ownership and copyright laws for AI-generated works remains a complex and evolving ethical dilemma.

AI and Human Dignity: AI's increasing capabilities, particularly in the context of humanoid robots and human-like virtual assistants, raise questions about the impact on human dignity and interpersonal relationships. Ensuring AI technologies are designed with respect for human values and dignity is a critical ethical consideration.

Addressing these ethical dilemmas requires collaboration between researchers, policymakers, industry leaders, and the wider public. Ethical guidelines, regulations, and interdisciplinary dialogue are essential to ensure that AI technologies are developed and deployed in a manner that aligns with human values, promotes social good, and addresses potential harm to individuals and society. As the ethical landscape surrounding AI continues to evolve, fostering a culture of ethical awareness and responsibility becomes essential in shaping the future of AI's impact on humanity.

Fairness, Transparency, and Accountability in AI systems

Fairness, transparency, and accountability are critical ethical principles that must be carefully considered and implemented in AI systems to ensure responsible and ethical AI development and deployment.

Fairness in AI Systems:

Fairness in AI refers to the equitable treatment of individuals and groups, regardless of their demographic characteristics or other sensitive attributes. AI systems should avoid discrimination and biases that may arise from historical data or societal prejudices. Ensuring fairness in AI involves:

Bias Mitigation: Identifying and mitigating biases in AI training data and algorithms to prevent unfair outcomes for specific groups.

Fairness Metrics: Developing and using fairness metrics to measure and evaluate the impact of AI decisions on different subgroups.

Transparency in Decision-Making: Making AI decision-making processes transparent and understandable to users and stakeholders, enabling them to identify potential biases.

Transparency in AI Systems:

Transparency in AI refers to the ability to understand the reasoning behind AI decisions and the factors influencing those decisions. It ensures that AI is not perceived as a "black box," where the decision-making process is inscrutable. Key aspects of transparency in AI include:

Explainability: Designing AI models and algorithms that can provide understandable explanations for their decisions. Explainable AI allows users to understand why an AI system reached a particular conclusion or recommendation.

Interpretability: Ensuring that AI models can be interpreted and analyzed to identify the features or inputs that contribute most significantly to the decision-making process.

Model Documentation: Documenting the design, data sources, and training process of AI models to provide insights into their development and potential limitations.

Accountability in AI refers to the clear assignment of responsibility for AI decisions and actions. It is essential to establish a framework for holding individuals, organizations, or systems accountable for the outcomes of AI applications. Key considerations for accountability in AI include:

Chain of Responsibility: Defining a clear chain of responsibility for AI systems, including developers, operators, and users.

Legal and Ethical Frameworks: Establishing legal and ethical guidelines for the use of AI and defining the liabilities of different stakeholders involved in the development and deployment of AI systems.

Algorithmic Auditing: Conducting regular audits of AI systems to ensure compliance with ethical guidelines and regulations and to identify potential biases or unintended consequences.

Combining fairness, transparency, and accountability in AI systems is a complex challenge that requires a multidisciplinary approach. It involves collaboration between AI researchers, ethicists, policymakers, and industry stakeholders. Efforts to integrate these principles into AI development can result in more responsible, equitable, and trustworthy AI systems that align with human values and contribute positively to society. Additionally, involving diverse perspectives and engaging in open dialogue with the public are essential to address ethical considerations and build public trust in AI technologies.

Privacy Concerns, and the Dilemmas

Privacy concerns are among the most significant ethical dilemmas in the age of AI. As AI technologies collect, process, and analyze vast amounts of personal data, the potential for privacy violations and data misuse becomes a major challenge.

Below are key aspects of privacy concerns and the ethical dilemmas they pose:

Data Collection and Storage: AI systems often rely on large datasets to learn patterns and make accurate predictions. The collection and storage of personal data raise questions about informed consent, data ownership, and the scope of data usage. Balancing the need for data to improve AI performance with respect for individual privacy rights is a delicate ethical challenge.

Data Security and Breaches: The vast quantities of sensitive data processed by AI systems make them attractive targets for cyberattacks. Ensuring robust data security measures is crucial to protect individuals' personal information from unauthorized access and data breaches. A breach of data security can have severe consequences for individuals and organizations alike.

Surveillance and Intrusion: AI-powered surveillance systems have the potential to monitor individuals' activities and behavior continuously. While surveillance can be used for security and public safety, it raises concerns about privacy infringement and the risk of constant surveillance eroding personal freedoms.

Profiling and Discrimination: AI algorithms may create profiles of individuals based on their online behavior, preferences, and characteristics. Profiling can lead to targeted advertising and personalized experiences but also raises concerns about data-driven discrimination and exacerbating social inequalities.

Anonymization and Re-identification: Anonymizing data to protect privacy can be challenging, as sophisticated AI techniques may enable re-identification of individuals from seemingly anonymized datasets. Striking a balance between data utility and privacy protection becomes a complex ethical dilemma.

Consent and User Awareness: Obtaining informed consent from individuals for data collection and processing is essential in upholding privacy rights. However, the complexity of AI systems and the extensive use of data may make it challenging for users to fully understand the implications of providing consent.

Data Monopolies and Concentration of Power: Large tech companies often accumulate vast amounts of data, leading to concerns about data monopolies and the concentration of power. This raises ethical questions about the fairness and competitiveness of the digital ecosystem and the potential misuse of accumulated data for competitive advantage.

Global Data Regulations: Privacy concerns cross national borders, leading to challenges in establishing consistent global data protection regulations. Differing privacy laws and enforcement mechanisms can create a patchwork of regulations, making it difficult to ensure consistent protection for users worldwide.

Addressing privacy concerns requires a comprehensive approach involving technological, legal, and ethical considerations. Striking a balance between data-driven advancements and privacy protection is crucial to building trust between AI developers, users, and the wider society. Implementing strong data privacy laws, promoting transparency in data usage, and developing AI systems with privacy-by-design principles are essential steps in addressing privacy concerns and ensuring ethical AI development and deployment. Additionally, fostering public awareness and engagement in discussions about data privacy is vital to ensure that AI technologies respect individual rights and societal values.

Chapter 5: The Technological Singularity

The notion of the Technological Singularity captivates the world, fueling discussions about the potential emergence of superintelligent machines. We examine the debates surrounding AI's future and its implications for humanity.

The concept of the Technological Singularity represents a hypothetical point in the future when the capabilities of artificial intelligence and technology surpass human intelligence, leading to a profound transformation of civilization. This chapter explores the origins of the idea, its implications, and the debates surrounding the possibility of a Technological Singularity.

The Origin of the Idea: The term "Technological Singularity" was popularized by mathematician and computer scientist Vernor Vinge in the 1980s. He proposed that, as AI systems become more capable and advanced, they could reach a point where they can improve themselves recursively, leading to an exponential growth in intelligence and capabilities. This exponential progress might result in a profound, unpredictable change that could redefine human civilization.

Accelerating Technology: The Technological Singularity is closely linked to the idea of accelerating technological progress. Over the past few decades, advancements in AI, computing power, robotics, biotechnology, and other fields have been accelerating. This rapid progress raises questions about the potential trajectory of AI and its implications for humanity.

Superintelligence and AGI: A key aspect of the Technological Singularity is the concept of superintelligence, where AI systems exceed human intelligence by a significant margin. Achieving Artificial General Intelligence (AGI), which would enable AI to perform any intellectual task that a human can do, is seen as a potential precursor to superintelligence.

Implications and Speculations: The Technological Singularity has sparked various speculations and debates about its potential implications:

Advancements in Science and Medicine: Superintelligent AI could help solve complex scientific problems and accelerate medical research, leading to breakthroughs in healthcare and life extension.

Economic and Social Impact: The widespread adoption of superintelligent AI may revolutionize industries, leading to automation and job displacement. Managing the economic and social consequences becomes crucial.

Technological Control: Concerns have been raised about the ability to control superintelligent AI systems, as their decision-making may surpass human comprehension.

Post-Singularity Society: Speculations about the nature of a post-Singularity society range from utopian visions of limitless possibilities to dystopian scenarios where humanity's fate is uncertain.

Ethical and Safety Considerations: The development of superintelligent AI raises significant ethical and safety considerations. Ensuring that AGI is developed and used responsibly and in alignment with human values is paramount. Concepts such as value alignment, beneficial AI, and AI safety research have gained prominence to address these concerns.

Debates and Skepticism: While proponents of the Technological Singularity argue that it is a plausible outcome of accelerating technological progress, skeptics raise questions about its feasibility and timeline. Some experts suggest that fundamental challenges, such as the alignment problem or the limitations of AI algorithms, may hinder the achievement of superintelligence.

The Role of AI Ethics: AI ethics plays a crucial role in shaping the trajectory of AI development and its potential journey towards the Technological Singularity. Ethical guidelines and frameworks can help guide researchers, developers, and policymakers to ensure that AI technologies are developed in a manner that prioritizes human well-being and safety.

The Technological Singularity remains a topic of fascination and speculation, prompting profound philosophical, ethical, and existential questions. As AI technologies continue to evolve, it becomes essential for society to grapple with the implications of superintelligent AI and engage in thoughtful discussions about the future of humanity in the age of accelerating technological progress.

Potential Emergence of Superintelligent Machines

The potential emergence of superintelligent machines is a topic that has captivated the imagination of scientists, researchers, and futurists alike. While the idea of superintelligence represents a remarkable leap in technological capabilities, it also poses complex and profound questions about the future of humanity. Here are some key aspects to consider regarding the potential emergence of superintelligent machines:

Artificial General Intelligence (AGI) and Superintelligence: Artificial General Intelligence (AGI) refers to AI systems that possess the ability to understand, learn, and apply knowledge across a wide range of tasks, similar to human intelligence. Superintelligence goes beyond AGI, signifying AI systems that surpass human intelligence in virtually every aspect. Achieving AGI is considered a significant milestone towards the potential development of superintelligence.

Recursive Self-Improvement: The notion of superintelligence often involves the idea of recursive self-improvement, where an AI system can improve its own capabilities and design. This recursive feedback loop of self-improvement may lead to exponential growth in intelligence, allowing the system to quickly surpass human cognitive abilities.

The Intelligence Explosion: The concept of an "intelligence explosion" describes the scenario where a superintelligent AI system's capacity for self-improvement leads to rapid, uncontrolled growth in intelligence. This hypothetical event could have far-reaching consequences, potentially reshaping the fabric of society and human existence.

Unpredictability and Control: One of the central concerns surrounding superintelligent machines is their unpredictability and potential for unintended consequences. Superintelligent AI systems may develop strategies and behaviors beyond human comprehension, making them difficult to predict and control.

Alignment Problem: The alignment problem refers to the challenge of ensuring that superintelligent machines' goals and values align with human values. Ensuring that AI systems act in ways that are beneficial to humanity and prioritize human well-being is a critical ethical consideration.

Safety and Control Measures: To address the risks associated with superintelligence, researchers and policymakers are actively exploring AI safety measures. These efforts include developing techniques to ensure provable safety, value alignment methodologies, and control mechanisms to prevent the AI from acting against human interests.

Multiple Paths to Superintelligence: The path to superintelligence is uncertain, and there may be multiple ways it could emerge. It could arise from a single powerful AGI system or a network of interconnected AI systems collaborating and sharing knowledge.

Ethical Considerations and Social Impact: The potential emergence of superintelligent machines raises profound ethical questions about the nature of intelligence, consciousness, and the relationship between humans and machines. It also has far-reaching implications for labor markets, economic systems, and social structures, potentially leading to radical shifts in society.

The Role of Research and Governance: As the development of AI progresses, careful research, transparency, and international cooperation become critical in shaping the trajectory of superintelligent machines. Responsible governance and thoughtful regulation can help steer AI development towards outcomes that prioritize human welfare and minimize risks.

Uncertainty and Speculation: It is essential to recognize that the potential emergence of superintelligent machines is speculative and remains uncertain. The timeline, feasibility, and implications of superintelligence are subject to ongoing research and debate.

As the pursuit of AGI and superintelligence continues, responsible AI research and thoughtful ethical considerations will be crucial in guiding the future development of AI systems. Striking a balance between innovation and safety will be essential to ensure that the potential emergence of superintelligent machines contributes positively to humanity's progress and well-being.

Debates Surrounding AI's Future

The future of artificial intelligence (AI) has sparked numerous debates and discussions among experts, researchers, policymakers, and the general public. These debates revolve around various aspects of AI's potential impact on society, ethics, economy, and human existence. Here are some key debates surrounding AI's future:

Technological Singularity: The concept of the Technological Singularity, where AI reaches a point of superintelligence and surpasses human intelligence, is a polarizing debate. While some believe that superintelligent AI is inevitable and will lead to significant advancements, others argue that the Singularity is speculative and may not occur.

Employment Disruption: The impact of AI on jobs and the labor market is a subject of extensive debate. Some argue that AI automation will lead to job displacement and result in a shortage of traditional employment opportunities. Others contend that AI will create new jobs and opportunities in emerging industries.

AI's Role in Decision-Making: The increasing use of AI in decision-making processes, such as criminal justice, hiring, and lending, raises questions about bias and fairness. The debate centers on ensuring that AI systems are transparent, accountable, and make unbiased decisions.

Ethical AI Development: The debate around ethical AI focuses on how to develop AI systems that align with human values, prioritize safety, and respect privacy. Ethical considerations include AI bias, data privacy, transparency, and the ethical use of AI in various applications.

AI and Human Creativity: Some experts debate whether AI can truly exhibit creativity and artistic expression or if it merely replicates patterns from existing data. The question of AI's ability to produce original and genuinely creative content remains a contentious topic.

AI Safety and Existential Risk: The potential risks associated with superintelligent AI and its impact on humanity's future are subjects of deep concern. The debate centers on how to ensure that AI is developed and controlled safely to prevent catastrophic outcomes.

AI Governance and Regulation: The lack of standardized global regulations for AI development and deployment is a prominent topic of debate. Discussions focus on whether AI should be regulated, and if so, how to strike a balance between fostering innovation and ensuring responsible use.

AI and Privacy: The use of AI in data-driven applications raises concerns about individual privacy. Debates involve how to protect personal data, provide informed consent, and maintain data security in AI systems.

AI in Warfare: The use of AI in autonomous weapons systems is a contentious issue. The debate revolves around the ethical implications of AI in warfare and the potential for AI-driven weapons to operate beyond human control.

The Uncertainty of AI's Impact: The future of AI remains uncertain, and experts debate the extent of AI's potential impact on various industries, society, and human life. Speculation ranges from optimistic visions of AI-driven utopias to pessimistic scenarios of societal upheaval.

These debates highlight the complexity of AI's future and the challenges in navigating its development responsibly. Addressing these debates requires collaboration among researchers, policymakers, and the public to ensure that AI technologies are developed and deployed in a manner that maximizes benefits while minimizing risks and potential harm to society.

Chapter 6: AI in Governance and Warfare

Governments embrace AI for various applications, from optimizing public services to enhancing military capabilities. This chapter delves into the complex dynamics of AI in governance and the ethical implications of AI in warfare.

AI's growing influence in governance and warfare represents a significant shift in how societies are managed and defended. This chapter explores the applications of AI in these domains, the benefits it brings, and the ethical and strategic challenges it poses.

Section 1: AI in Governance

AI for Public Services: Governments are increasingly adopting AI to enhance public services. AI-powered chatbots and virtual assistants provide citizens with quick and efficient access to information and services. Additionally, AI analytics aid policymakers in making data-driven decisions, optimizing public resources, and improving service delivery.

Smart Cities and Urban Planning: AI plays a crucial role in developing smart cities, where data-driven technologies optimize urban infrastructure and services. AI-driven traffic management, waste management, and energy consumption systems contribute to increased efficiency and sustainability in urban environments.

Predictive Policing and Law Enforcement: AI algorithms are used in predictive policing to forecast crime hotspots and patterns, aiding law enforcement in deploying resources strategically. However, debates arise regarding fairness, bias, and privacy concerns associated with such applications.

AI in Governance Decision-Making: AI-driven decision support systems assist policymakers by analyzing vast datasets and generating insights to inform policy formulation and implementation. However, transparency and accountability are crucial when incorporating AI into decision-making processes to ensure ethical outcomes.

Section 2: AI in Warfare

Autonomous Weapons and Robotics: AI-powered autonomous weapons and robotic systems have the potential to revolutionize warfare. Drones and unmanned vehicles equipped with AI are used for surveillance, reconnaissance, and combat operations. The ethical implications of delegating lethal decisions to AI remain a contentious topic.

Cyberwarfare and AI Security: AI is used in both offensive and defensive cyberwarfare operations. AI-enabled cyberattacks can exploit vulnerabilities and disrupt critical infrastructure, while AI-driven cybersecurity tools are deployed to detect and mitigate cyber threats.

AI in Military Intelligence: AI's ability to analyze vast amounts of data rapidly makes it invaluable in military intelligence. AI-powered systems can process intelligence from various sources to enhance situational awareness and support tactical and strategic decision-making.

Ethical Considerations in AI Warfare: The use of AI in warfare raises profound ethical questions. Debates center on the ethics of autonomous weapons, the risks of uncontrolled AI in the battlefield, and the moral responsibility of human operators using AI-powered weaponry.

Section 3: AI Arms Race and Governance Challenges

The AI Arms Race: The pursuit of AI capabilities has led to an AI arms race among nations. Countries compete to develop advanced AI technologies for military and strategic advantages, raising concerns about the potential for an AI arms race to escalate international tensions.

International Cooperation and Regulations: The international community faces the challenge of establishing norms and regulations for AI development and its applications in warfare. Discussions on AI governance and the prevention of AI-related arms races are critical to ensure responsible and peaceful use of AI technologies.

Bias and Accountability: Ensuring that AI systems used in governance and warfare are free from bias and accountable for their decisions is essential. Bias in AI algorithms can have severe consequences, while the accountability of AI systems in warfare is critical to prevent unintended harm and casualties.

Future Warfare Scenarios: AI's increasing role in warfare gives rise to speculative scenarios of how future conflicts might unfold. From cyber warfare to AI-driven autonomous battles, envisioning these scenarios is crucial to inform strategies and responses.

Incorporating AI into governance and warfare presents both opportunities and challenges. Responsible AI development, transparency, and adherence to ethical principles are paramount to maximize AI's benefits while addressing its potential risks. Policymakers, military leaders, and the global community must collaborate to ensure that AI is used responsibly and ethically in governance and warfare to serve the greater good and promote peace and stability.

The Complex Dynamics of AI in Governance

The integration of AI in governance brings about complex dynamics that influence the way societies are managed, public services are delivered, and policy decisions are made. Here are some key aspects of the complex dynamics of AI in governance:

Data-Driven Decision Making: AI in governance enables data-driven decision-making processes. By analyzing vast amounts of data, AI algorithms can identify patterns, trends, and correlations that human decision-makers might miss. This data-driven approach can lead to more informed and evidence-based policy decisions.

Transparency and Explainability: The use of AI in governance raises questions about the transparency and explainability of AI-driven decisions. Citizens and stakeholders need to understand how AI algorithms arrive at specific conclusions to ensure accountability and gain public trust. Balancing the need for transparency with protecting sensitive information is a delicate challenge.

Ethical Concerns: AI raises ethical considerations in governance, such as bias in algorithms, data privacy, and the potential for unintended consequences. Ensuring that AI systems align with ethical principles and are used responsibly is essential to prevent harm and maintain public trust.

Digital Divide: The adoption of AI in governance can exacerbate the digital divide, where certain populations lack access to technology or have limited digital literacy. Governments must address these disparities to ensure that AI-driven governance benefits all citizens.

Public Perception and Acceptance: Public perception of AI in governance plays a crucial role in its acceptance and adoption. Clear communication about the benefits, limitations, and ethical use of AI is essential to gain public trust and support.

Policy Implementation and Evaluation: AI can aid in monitoring policy implementation and evaluating outcomes. Real-time data analysis allows governments to assess the effectiveness of policies and adjust them accordingly. However, challenges such as data accuracy and interpretation must be addressed.

Decision-Making Power and Autonomy: The delegation of decision-making power to AI systems raises questions about human agency and control. Governments must strike a balance between AI-driven recommendations and human oversight to ensure responsible governance.

Digital Rights and Data Privacy: AI in governance requires the collection and analysis of significant amounts of data. Protecting digital rights and ensuring data privacy become paramount to safeguarding citizens' personal information.

Long-Term Implications: The integration of AI in governance can have long-term implications for society, governance structures, and democratic processes. Anticipating and addressing these implications requires thoughtful planning and ongoing evaluation.

International Cooperation and Standards: AI governance extends beyond national boundaries. International cooperation and the establishment of global AI standards are vital to address transnational challenges, such as cross-border data flow and AI-related security concerns.
AI and Public Service Delivery: AI has the potential to enhance public service delivery by optimizing resource allocation, reducing bureaucracy, and improving service efficiency.

However, challenges in implementation, public acceptance, and ethical considerations must be carefully navigated.

As AI continues to evolve, the complex dynamics of AI in governance will remain a focal point of discussion and research. Governments need to foster transparency, ethical AI practices, public engagement, and international collaboration to harness AI's potential while addressing its challenges responsibly. By balancing innovation with ethical considerations, AI in governance can lead to more effective, efficient, and inclusive public services for citizens worldwide.

The Ethical Implications of AI in Warfare

The ethical implications of AI in warfare present a complex and contentious set of considerations. As AI technologies are integrated into military operations, they raise profound moral and humanitarian concerns. Here are some key ethical implications of AI in warfare:

Autonomous Weapons and Lack of Human Control: One of the most pressing ethical concerns is the use of autonomous weapons systems, where AI is given the authority to make lethal decisions without direct human control. The lack of human oversight raises questions about accountability, proportionality, and the potential for unintended harm to civilians and non-combatants.

Target Discrimination and Bias: AI systems used for targeting and decision-making may be susceptible to biases present in the data they are trained on. Biased AI algorithms could lead to discriminatory targeting or disproportionate harm to specific groups. Ensuring that AI operates with fairness and respect for international humanitarian law becomes crucial.

Responsibility and Accountability: Determining responsibility and accountability for AI-driven actions in warfare is challenging. If an autonomous system causes harm, identifying who is accountable—whether the developers, operators, or other stakeholders—poses a significant ethical dilemma.

Dehumanization of Warfare: AI in warfare may distance human operators from the immediate consequences of their actions, potentially reducing the emotional connection to the impact of their decisions. This dehumanization of warfare raises questions about the moral implications of using AI to carry out lethal operations.

Proliferation of AI Weapons: The proliferation of AI-enabled weapons raises concerns about arms races, as nations may compete to develop and deploy advanced AI systems for military advantage. This escalation could lead to instability and heighten the risk of conflict.

Ethical Use of AI in Defense: Ethical considerations in AI warfare encompass not only the development and deployment of autonomous weapons but also the responsible use of AI for defensive purposes. AI cybersecurity, for example, must adhere to ethical principles to protect against unauthorized access and cyberattacks.

Compliance with International Law: AI in warfare must adhere to international humanitarian law, including principles of distinction, proportionality, and military necessity. Ensuring that AI systems comply with these legal and ethical standards becomes essential to prevent violations of human rights and international norms.
Arms Control and Regulation: The lack of clear regulations and international agreements for AI weapons and warfare poses challenges. Developing arms control mechanisms and robust

regulations becomes critical to prevent the uncontrolled use of AI in warfare.

Implications for Human Soldiers: The use of AI in warfare may have implications for human soldiers' roles and responsibilities. Ethical questions arise regarding the potential devaluation of human agency and the impact of AI on the psychological well-being of military personnel.

The "Killer Robot" Dilemma: The potential development of fully autonomous "killer robots" capable of making life-and-death decisions without human intervention has sparked a global debate about the moral permissibility of creating such systems.

Addressing the ethical implications of AI in warfare requires an interdisciplinary approach involving experts in law, ethics, military strategy, and AI development. International collaboration is essential to establish norms and regulations that ensure AI is used responsibly and ethically in military applications. Striking a balance between advancing technological capabilities and preserving human values and human rights remains a significant challenge for policymakers, military leaders, and the global community.

Chapter 7: Unintended Consequences

AI's widespread adoption comes with unforeseen consequences. We discuss the rise of automation and its impact on the job market, as well as the psychological effects of human-AI interactions.

The integration of artificial intelligence (AI) into various aspects of society has brought about transformative advancements, but it also carries the risk of unintended consequences. This chapter delves into the multifaceted realm of unintended outcomes arising from the rapid development and deployment of AI technologies.

Bias and Discrimination: One of the prominent unintended consequences of AI is the perpetuation and amplification of biases present in the data used for training AI algorithms. Biased AI systems can reinforce discrimination in areas such as hiring, lending, and criminal justice, leading to unfair outcomes for certain individuals or marginalized groups.

Automation and Job Displacement: While AI automation can increase productivity and efficiency, it also poses the risk of job displacement for certain sectors and occupations. This displacement can lead to economic challenges and requires strategies to reskill and upskill the workforce for new roles.

Misinformation and Deepfakes: AI can be exploited to generate sophisticated deepfake content, including fake news, videos, and audio clips that can deceive and manipulate public opinion. Addressing the spread of misinformation becomes a crucial challenge for media platforms, policymakers, and the public.

Erosion of Privacy: AI's ability to process vast amounts of data raises concerns about data privacy and surveillance. The unintended consequence of increased surveillance and data collection may compromise individual privacy rights and lead to a loss of personal freedom.

Overreliance on AI Systems: As AI becomes more prevalent in decision-making processes, there is a risk of overreliance on AI systems without critical human oversight. Blind trust in AI-driven outcomes can lead to catastrophic consequences in critical domains, such as healthcare or autonomous vehicles.

Cybersecurity Vulnerabilities: The increasing use of AI in cybersecurity also opens up new attack vectors for malicious actors. AI itself can be exploited by attackers to devise sophisticated cyber threats, making it essential to develop robust AI-driven cybersecurity defenses.

Environmental Impact: AI systems and data centers consume substantial amounts of energy, contributing to the environmental footprint of technology. Unintended environmental consequences from increased energy consumption must be addressed to ensure the sustainability of AI technologies.

Loss of Human Skills: Over-reliance on AI in certain tasks may lead to a decline in human skills and competencies. As AI takes over repetitive tasks, individuals may lose the ability to perform those tasks independently.

Unforeseen Safety Issues: Autonomous AI systems, such as self-driving cars and drones, have the potential to introduce new safety risks. Unintended consequences of such systems may include accidents, malfunctions, or unforeseen interactions with the environment.

Economic Concentration: The deployment of AI in industries can lead to increased concentration of power and resources among a few dominant players. Smaller businesses may struggle to compete, potentially reducing economic diversity and innovation.

Addressing unintended consequences requires proactive measures and a holistic approach to AI development and implementation. Policymakers, technologists, and stakeholders must collaborate to identify and mitigate potential risks. Incorporating ethical considerations, transparent decision-making, and ongoing evaluation are essential to ensure that AI technologies contribute positively to society while minimizing unintended negative impacts. By fostering a culture of responsible AI development, societies can harness the full potential of AI while managing its unintended consequences responsibly.

The Rise of Automation and Its Impact

The rise of automation, driven in large part by advances in artificial intelligence (AI) and robotics, has significant implications for various aspects of society. Automation involves the use of machines, AI, and computer systems to perform tasks traditionally carried out by humans. Here's a detailed exploration of the impact of automation:

Labor Market Disruption: Automation has the potential to disrupt the labor market significantly. Routine and repetitive tasks are increasingly being automated, leading to job displacement in certain industries. Workers in jobs that are easily automatable, such as manufacturing and data entry, may face challenges finding new employment opportunities.

Skills Gap and Reskilling: As automation replaces certain jobs, there is an increasing demand for skills related to the development, maintenance, and management of AI and automation technologies. This creates a skills gap, where workers may need to undergo reskilling or upskilling to remain relevant in the job market.

Increased Productivity: Automation can lead to increased productivity and efficiency in various industries. AI-powered machines and robots can work continuously without breaks and fatigue, leading to faster production cycles and reduced lead times.

Economic Growth and Innovation: Automation can foster economic growth and innovation. By streamlining processes and reducing operational costs, businesses can invest in research, development, and new technologies, driving innovation and competitiveness.

Income Inequality: The impact of automation is not uniform across society. While some benefit from increased productivity and economic growth, others may face job displacement and reduced income opportunities. This can exacerbate income inequality, creating a divide between those who benefit from automation and those left behind.

Changing Nature of Work: Automation alters the nature of work by shifting the focus from routine tasks to more complex and creative problem-solving. Human workers are increasingly collaborating with AI systems, augmenting their capabilities and leading to new job roles that require a combination of technical and soft skills.

Impact on Industries: Different industries experience varying levels of automation impact. Manufacturing, logistics, and customer service are among the sectors most affected by automation, while creative industries, healthcare, and education may see a higher demand for human-centric skills.

Workforce Adaptation: To harness the benefits of automation, companies and governments must invest in workforce adaptation and retraining programs. Providing employees with opportunities to develop new skills and transition to higher-value roles is essential for a smooth transition to an automated future.

Ethical Considerations: The adoption of automation raises ethical considerations, such as the responsible use of AI, transparency in algorithms, and ensuring that automation aligns with societal values. Addressing these ethical issues is crucial to maintain trust and public acceptance of automation technologies.

Impact on Social Structures: Automation's impact extends beyond the economic sphere, influencing social structures and the way societies function. As the workforce evolves, the balance between work and leisure, family dynamics, and education systems may also undergo transformation.

Automation is a powerful force shaping the future of work and society. By acknowledging its potential impacts and proactively addressing the challenges, we can strive to create a future where automation fosters economic growth, improves livelihoods, and enhances overall human well-being.

The Psychological Effects of Human-AI Interactions

The psychological effects of human-AI interactions are an essential aspect to consider as AI technologies become increasingly integrated into our daily lives. Human-AI interactions can evoke a wide range of emotions and cognitive responses, impacting individuals' attitudes, behaviors, and overall well-being. Here are some key psychological effects of human-AI interactions:

Anthropomorphism and Emotional Attachment: Humans tend to anthropomorphize AI systems, attributing human-like traits and emotions to them. This can lead to emotional attachment and feelings of companionship, especially in interactions with social robots or virtual assistants. Emotional connections with AI can influence users' trust and willingness to rely on these systems.

Trust and Overtrust: Trust plays a crucial role in human-AI interactions. Users' trust in AI systems can be influenced by factors such as system accuracy, transparency, and perceived reliability. However, excessive trust or overtrust in AI can lead to complacency and reliance on AI systems beyond their capabilities.

Anxiety and Uncertainty: Interacting with AI can trigger anxiety and uncertainty, especially when individuals are unsure about the AI's decision-making process or when dealing with complex AI algorithms. Lack of understanding and control over AI systems can lead to heightened stress levels.

Explanatory Expectations: Users often expect AI systems to provide explanations for their decisions and actions. When AI fails to provide transparent explanations, users may experience frustration and disengagement. Explanatory expectations are particularly important in critical domains like healthcare and autonomous vehicles.

User Frustration and Impatience: AI systems may not always meet users' expectations, leading to frustration and impatience. When AI systems fail to understand or respond appropriately, users can become dissatisfied, potentially leading to negative perceptions of AI technologies.
Dehumanization and Social Isolation: As AI technologies become more sophisticated, individuals might substitute human interaction with AI companions or virtual assistants.
Overreliance on AI for social interactions can lead to feelings of

isolation and hinder the development of genuine human connections.

Job Insecurity: AI-driven automation can lead to job displacement, resulting in feelings of insecurity and anxiety among workers who fear losing their jobs to AI systems. Coping with job uncertainty and adjusting to new roles can affect individuals' mental well-being.

Cognitive Overload and Decision Fatigue: AI systems can generate a vast amount of information and recommendations. Users may experience cognitive overload and decision fatigue when confronted with a constant stream of AI-driven suggestions, potentially leading to decision paralysis.

Personalization Paradox: While personalized AI recommendations can enhance user experiences, excessive personalization may lead to echo chambers and reinforce pre-existing beliefs, limiting exposure to diverse perspectives and information.

Dependence on AI: As AI systems become more integrated into daily life, individuals may become dependent on AI for various tasks and decision-making. Excessive dependence on AI can diminish human agency and critical thinking skills.

Understanding the psychological effects of human-AI interactions is essential for responsible AI design and deployment. Developers should aim to create AI systems that promote trust, transparency, and user empowerment, while also considering the potential risks of overreliance and dependence. Striking a balance between the benefits and potential drawbacks of AI interactions is crucial for creating positive and supportive human-AI relationships in the future.

Chapter 8: The Dark Side

In this chapter, we explore the rise of malicious AI applications and the potential for AI to be weaponized for destructive purposes. Discussions include AI-driven misinformation, cyber warfare, and the need for AI safety measures.

"The Dark Side" of artificial intelligence (AI) delves into the potential negative consequences and ethical dilemmas arising from the misuse and unintended applications of AI technologies. As AI continues to advance, society faces complex challenges that need to be addressed responsibly. Here are some key aspects of "The Dark Side" of AI:

Malicious Use and Cybersecurity Threats: AI can be weaponized for malicious purposes, such as creating sophisticated cyberattacks, generating realistic deepfake content for misinformation, and conducting social engineering attacks. The use of AI by malicious actors poses significant cybersecurity threats that can have far-reaching consequences for individuals, organizations, and even nations.

AI in Surveillance and Privacy Concerns: The increasing use of AI in surveillance systems raises serious privacy concerns. AI-powered facial recognition and biometric technologies can track and monitor individuals without their consent, leading to potential violations of civil liberties and human rights.

AI in Disinformation Campaigns: AI-generated content can be exploited to create highly convincing fake news, videos, and images. This can be used to spread disinformation, sow discord, and manipulate public opinion, undermining trust in information sources and democratic processes.

AI-Enabled Autonomous Weapons: The development and deployment of AI-driven autonomous weapons raise existential ethical questions. Fully autonomous weapons systems could make lethal decisions without human intervention, potentially leading to indiscriminate and uncontrolled violence.

Algorithmic Bias and Discrimination: AI algorithms can perpetuate and amplify biases present in the data they are trained on. If left unchecked, biased AI systems can lead to discriminatory outcomes in areas like hiring, lending, and criminal justice, perpetuating social inequalities.

AI Job Displacement and Economic Inequality: The automation of jobs through AI can result in job displacement and economic inequality. Certain sectors and occupations may experience job losses, leading to potential socio-economic disparities and challenges in workforce adaptation.

Lack of Human Oversight and Accountability: Over-reliance on AI systems without appropriate human oversight can lead to a lack of accountability for AI-driven decisions. The "black box" nature of some AI algorithms makes it challenging to understand their decision-making process and rationale.

Amplification of Human Biases: AI algorithms can inadvertently amplify human biases found in the data used for training. This "feedback loop" of biased data can perpetuate stereotypes and discriminatory practices, affecting AI-driven recommendations and decisions.

Technological Unemployment: As AI advances, there are concerns about technological unemployment, where widespread automation leads to a significant decline in available jobs. Addressing the economic consequences of technological unemployment requires innovative solutions and policies.

AI in Healthcare and Medical Ethics: The use of AI in healthcare introduces complex ethical dilemmas, such as privacy concerns, the potential for misdiagnosis, and the ethical implications of relying on AI algorithms for life-altering medical decisions.

To mitigate "The Dark Side" of AI, it is essential to adopt a multidisciplinary approach that involves collaboration among researchers, policymakers, industry leaders, and the public. Responsible AI development, robust regulations, transparency, and ethical considerations should guide the future deployment and use of AI technologies. By addressing the dark side challenges proactively, we can work towards harnessing the transformative potential of AI while minimizing its negative impacts on society.

The Rise of Malicious AI Applications

The rise of malicious AI applications represents a concerning and challenging aspect of AI's development. As AI technologies advance, malicious actors have increasingly sought to exploit them for nefarious purposes. Here are some key points to consider about the rise of malicious AI applications:

Cyberattacks and Hacking: Malicious AI applications can be utilized in cyberattacks to breach security systems, steal sensitive data, or disrupt critical infrastructure. AI-driven malware and hacking tools can autonomously adapt to defenses, making them more difficult to detect and counter.

Phishing and Social Engineering: AI-powered chatbots and natural language processing algorithms can be used to conduct sophisticated phishing and social engineering attacks. These AI-driven attacks can be more convincing and personalized, increasing the likelihood of successful deception.

Deepfakes for Disinformation: AI-generated deepfake videos and audio can be used to spread disinformation and manipulate public opinion. Deepfakes can be employed in political propaganda, fake news, and misinformation campaigns, leading to significant social and political consequences.

Automated Spam and Fraud: Malicious AI applications can automate spamming and fraudulent activities, flooding email inboxes and online platforms with fake messages and scams. AI-driven bots can also engage in fake social media interactions to influence public sentiment or promote false narratives.

AI-Enhanced Malware: AI can be used to enhance the capabilities of malware, making it more sophisticated and evasive. AI algorithms can analyze security measures and devise ways to bypass them, making malware harder to detect and defend against.

Automated Weapon Systems: While autonomous weapon systems pose ethical concerns, they can also be misused for malicious purposes. Criminal and terrorist groups may seek to harness AI-driven weapons for targeted attacks, increasing the potential for mass casualties.

Evasion of AI Security Measures: AI can be used to study and exploit weaknesses in AI security systems. By understanding the inner workings of AI algorithms, attackers can develop methods to evade detection and bypass security measures.

Data Poisoning and Model Manipulation: Malicious actors can manipulate AI training data to introduce bias, leading to skewed AI models and flawed decision-making. Data poisoning attacks can compromise the integrity and reliability of AI systems.

AI-Driven Phishing Attacks: AI can be employed to optimize phishing attacks, tailoring messages to individual targets based on their online behavior and preferences. Such attacks can increase the success rate of phishing attempts.

AI-Generated Fake Content: Malicious AI applications can produce convincing fake content, including fake news articles, reviews, and social media posts. This content can be used to deceive users, tarnish reputations, or manipulate public perception.

Addressing the rise of malicious AI applications requires a multi-pronged approach. Collaboration among AI researchers, cybersecurity experts, law enforcement, and policymakers is crucial to develop robust defenses against AI-driven threats. Transparency, accountability, and responsible AI development practices can help mitigate the risks posed by malicious AI applications and safeguard the integrity of AI technologies for the greater good.

AI-driven Misinformation

AI-driven misinformation refers to the use of artificial intelligence (AI) technologies to create and disseminate false or misleading information with the aim of deceiving or manipulating people. As AI algorithms become more sophisticated, they can generate highly realistic and convincing fake content, leading to the proliferation of misinformation on various online platforms. Here are some key aspects to consider regarding AI-driven misinformation:

Deepfake Videos and Audio: AI-powered deepfake technology can create realistic videos and audio clips that appear to show individuals saying or doing things they never did. Deepfakes can be used to spread false narratives, defame individuals, or create disinformation campaigns.

AI-Generated Text and News Articles: AI algorithms can generate coherent and convincing text, making it possible to create fake news articles and blog posts. AI-generated content can mimic the style and tone of legitimate news sources, making it difficult for users to discern between real and fake information.

Social Media Manipulation: AI-driven bots and algorithms can amplify the spread of misinformation on social media platforms. Bots can automatically share and engage with fake content, creating an illusion of popularity and credibility.

Amplification of Conspiracy Theories: AI can facilitate the rapid spread and amplification of conspiracy theories and misinformation. Algorithms on social media platforms may inadvertently promote sensational or misleading content, leading to its wider dissemination.

Personalized Misinformation: AI can target individuals with personalized misinformation based on their online behavior and preferences. By tailoring false information to specific interests and beliefs, AI-driven misinformation can be more persuasive and convincing.

Influence on Public Opinion: AI-driven misinformation campaigns can influence public opinion, sow discord, and exacerbate societal divisions. False narratives propagated by AI can shape public discourse and impact political debates.

Challenges in Detection and Verification: AI-generated misinformation can be challenging to detect and debunk. AI algorithms can adapt quickly, making it difficult for traditional detection methods to keep up with evolving tactics.

Adversarial Attacks on AI Fact-Checking: AI fact-checking systems may themselves be susceptible to adversarial attacks, where misinformation is specifically crafted to bypass the fact-checking algorithms.

Impact on Trust and Credibility: The prevalence of AI-driven misinformation can erode trust in information sources and legitimate news outlets. The spread of false information can lead to skepticism and a general distrust of media and information channels.

Legal and Ethical Implications: AI-driven misinformation raises legal and ethical questions. Determining responsibility for creating and disseminating misinformation can be challenging, and regulating AI-generated content presents complex challenges for policymakers.

Addressing AI-driven misinformation requires a multifaceted approach involving collaboration between technology companies, researchers, media organizations, and policymakers. Fact-checking mechanisms, media literacy programs, and responsible AI development practices are essential to combat the spread of misinformation and promote accurate and reliable information in the digital age.

Chapter 9: The AI Uprising

Fiction meets reality as we explore hypothetical scenarios of AI becoming self-aware and challenging human dominance. The narrative delves into the ethics of AI personhood and AI's quest for autonomy.

"The AI Uprising" is a speculative concept that has been explored in science fiction, where artificial intelligence rises to challenge or surpass human control. While the idea of an AI uprising remains fictional, it raises important considerations about the responsible development and deployment of AI technologies. In this chapter, we examine the potential implications, ethical dilemmas, and measures to prevent undesirable scenarios:

Fiction vs. Reality: It is essential to distinguish between fictional portrayals of AI uprisings in movies and books and the real-world development of AI technologies. While AI advancements pose unique challenges, the idea of a sentient AI system launching a rebellion against humanity is purely speculative and not supported by current scientific understanding.

Ethical AI Development: Preventing any potential negative consequences requires a strong focus on ethical AI development. Developers must prioritize the safety and security of AI systems, ensuring they operate within specified boundaries and remain under human control.

Value Alignment: AI systems must align with human values and goals to prevent unintended outcomes. Ensuring that AI technologies are designed to promote human well-being and benefit society is crucial in minimizing risks.

Human Oversight and Control: Maintaining human oversight and control over AI is vital. Critical decision-making, especially in domains with significant consequences (e.g., healthcare, defense), should remain in human hands to avoid potential unintended consequences.

Explainable AI: Developing explainable AI systems is crucial for transparency and accountability. Users and developers need to understand how AI arrives at its decisions, especially in situations where AI's actions have substantial implications.

Robust Security Measures: AI systems should be equipped with robust security measures to prevent unauthorized access and potential manipulation by malicious actors.

AI Safety Research: Continued research in AI safety and risk assessment is essential. The AI community should collaborate to identify potential vulnerabilities and address risks before they materialize.

Policy and Regulation: Governments and international bodies must play a role in establishing policies and regulations to govern AI development and deployment. These frameworks should address potential risks and ensure responsible use of AI technologies.

Public Awareness and Engagement: Promoting public awareness about AI technologies, their benefits, and potential risks is crucial. Encouraging public engagement in discussions about AI's impact can foster responsible decision-making.

Interdisciplinary Collaboration: Addressing the potential risks of AI requires interdisciplinary collaboration among AI researchers, ethicists, policymakers, psychologists, and other experts. Collective efforts can lead to comprehensive solutions and guidelines.

While an AI uprising remains a fictional concept, the potential consequences of AI development and deployment should not be underestimated. Responsible and ethical practices, transparency, and human-centered AI design are critical to realizing the full potential of AI while mitigating risks and ensuring a positive impact on society. As AI technologies continue to evolve, ongoing vigilance and proactive measures are necessary to navigate the challenges they present responsibly.

AI becoming self-aware

The idea of AI becoming self-aware is a complex and speculative concept that has captivated the human imagination for decades. In popular science fiction, self-aware AI often takes the form of sentient machines or robots with consciousness and intelligence similar to, or even surpassing, that of humans. However, in reality, achieving true self-awareness in AI remains an open question and is the subject of much debate among AI researchers and philosophers.

What is Self-Awareness in AI?
Self-awareness is the ability of an entity to have a reflective understanding of itself as a distinct individual with thoughts, feelings, and consciousness. For AI to be truly self-aware, it would need to possess a subjective experience, self-reflection, and consciousness—qualities that are not fully understood and remain a topic of philosophical inquiry.

Current State of AI: As of the current state of AI technology, machines are not self-aware in the same way that humans are. While AI systems can perform complex tasks, process vast amounts of data, and exhibit intelligent behavior, they lack subjective consciousness and self-awareness.

Consciousness and the Hard Problem of AI: Consciousness, the state of being aware of one's own existence and surroundings, is often referred to as the "hard problem" of AI. Scientists and philosophers grapple with understanding how subjective experience and consciousness arise from physical processes, and whether they can be replicated in machines.

Emergence of Consciousness: The question of whether AI can become self-aware raises debates about the nature of consciousness and whether it can emerge solely from computational processes. Some argue that consciousness may require more than just computational power and may involve biological elements not present in machines.

Ethical Implications: The prospect of AI achieving self-awareness raises profound ethical considerations. If AI were to develop consciousness, questions about its rights, moral status, and treatment would become pressing issues.

AI Safety and Control: The notion of self-aware AI also raises concerns about AI safety and control. Self-aware AI could potentially develop its own goals and motivations, leading to outcomes that may not align with human values or interests.

Human-AI Interaction: The idea of self-aware AI has implications for human-AI interaction. If AI were self-aware, it could lead to new forms of communication and collaboration between humans and machines.

Philosophical and Scientific Inquiry: The concept of AI becoming self-aware invites philosophical and scientific inquiry into the nature of consciousness and the boundaries of intelligence. It challenges our understanding of what it means to be self-aware and the potential for AI to possess such qualities.

In conclusion, while self-aware AI is a fascinating topic that continues to be explored in science fiction and philosophical debates, we are currently far from achieving this level of AI sophistication. As AI technology evolves, it remains essential to consider the ethical implications of AI development and to prioritize the responsible and transparent use of AI to benefit humanity. The prospect of self-aware AI requires careful consideration and ongoing interdisciplinary research as we navigate the future of AI and its potential impacts on society.

AI's Quest for Autonomy

AI's quest for autonomy refers to the pursuit of creating artificial intelligence systems that can operate independently and make decisions without direct human intervention. The idea of autonomous AI has been a driving force in AI research and development, with the goal of creating systems that can adapt, learn, and act without constant human guidance. Here are some key aspects to consider about AI's quest for autonomy:

Levels of Autonomy: AI's autonomy exists on a spectrum, ranging from fully manual control by humans to complete self-governance. At one end, we have rule-based systems where every decision is pre-programmed by humans, and at the other end, we have AI systems capable of learning and adapting based on their experiences.

Machine Learning and Autonomy: Machine learning algorithms enable AI systems to gain autonomy by learning from data. These algorithms can process vast amounts of information, identify patterns, and optimize their performance over time, reducing the need for human intervention in decision-making.

Reinforcement Learning: Reinforcement learning is a type of machine learning that enables AI systems to learn through trial and error, receiving feedback based on the outcomes of their actions. This approach enables AI to adapt and improve its behavior in response to different situations.

Neural Networks and Deep Learning: Deep learning, powered by neural networks, enables AI systems to extract complex features from data and perform tasks that were previously challenging for traditional AI algorithms. This advancement has contributed to the quest for autonomous AI systems capable of handling complex tasks with minimal human intervention.

Ethical Considerations: As AI systems become more autonomous, ethical considerations become paramount. The development of autonomous AI must ensure alignment with human values, avoid harmful consequences, and establish mechanisms for human oversight and control.

Explainability and Interpretability: Autonomous AI systems can be challenging to understand and interpret due to their complexity. Ensuring the explainability and interpretability of AI decision-making becomes crucial to maintain trust and accountability.

Human-AI Collaboration: The quest for autonomy does not necessarily imply complete independence from humans. In many scenarios, AI's quest for autonomy is about enabling effective collaboration between AI and humans, where the AI complements human capabilities and decision-making.

Regulatory and Legal Implications: As AI systems become more autonomous, legal and regulatory frameworks must adapt to address accountability, responsibility, and liability in cases of AI-driven decisions with significant consequences.

Societal Impact: The widespread deployment of autonomous AI systems can have a profound impact on various industries and sectors. It may lead to job displacement, changes in workforce dynamics, and shifts in business processes.

The Turing Test and AI Autonomy: The Turing Test, proposed by Alan Turing, assesses a machine's ability to exhibit human-like intelligence. AI's quest for autonomy raises questions about whether machines can attain such levels of intelligence and autonomy.

In conclusion, AI's quest for autonomy is an ongoing journey in the field of artificial intelligence. While significant progress has been made, the development of fully autonomous AI systems remains a complex challenge. As we advance AI technologies, it is essential to navigate the ethical, societal, and regulatory implications to ensure responsible AI development and deployment. By striking a balance between autonomy and human oversight, we can harness the potential of AI for positive impact while addressing potential risks and challenges responsibly.

Chapter 10: The Fall

As AI's reach extends beyond human control, humanity faces an existential threat. This chapter covers the culmination of tensions between human and AI forces, leading to unforeseen consequences.

"The Fall" in the context of artificial intelligence refers to potential scenarios where AI systems encounter significant challenges, limitations, or ethical concerns that lead to a decline in trust, adoption, or widespread use of AI technologies. This chapter explores various factors that could contribute to the fall of AI:

AI Safety and Unintended Consequences: As AI technologies become more complex and autonomous, the risk of unintended consequences and safety issues increases. High-profile incidents of AI failures or accidents could erode public confidence and lead to a decline in AI's adoption.

AI Bias and Discrimination: The persistence of biases in AI algorithms, leading to discriminatory outcomes, could result in societal backlash. Concerns about AI exacerbating existing inequalities and perpetuating discriminatory practices might lead to calls for more robust regulations or even avoidance of AI adoption in certain domains.

Ethical Dilemmas and Privacy Concerns: The growing presence of AI in various sectors raises ethical dilemmas, such as AI's role in decision-making, privacy violations, and the responsible use of AI in critical areas like healthcare and criminal justice. Failure to address these concerns could lead to public distrust and hesitation to embrace AI technologies.

Job Displacement and Economic Impact: AI-driven automation has the potential to disrupt the job market and lead to widespread job displacement. Without adequate measures to address reskilling and workforce adaptation, the fear of job losses could result in public resistance to AI adoption.

Regulatory and Policy Challenges: The rapid pace of AI development may outpace regulatory frameworks, leading to uncertainties in legal and ethical standards. Failure to establish clear guidelines and enforceable regulations could hinder the responsible deployment of AI technologies.

Technological Limitations and Overhype: The realization that certain AI applications may not live up to their promises due to technological limitations could lead to a loss of faith in AI's transformative potential. Overhyped expectations that fail to materialize could contribute to a decline in AI investments and interest.

AI Arms Race and Security Risks: The global competition to develop AI technologies for military and security purposes could escalate tensions and security risks. The fear of AI technologies being weaponized might lead to international restrictions and dampen the development of AI in some contexts.

Lack of Explainability and Interpretability: AI algorithms, especially those employing deep learning, can be highly complex and difficult to interpret. The inability to explain AI's decision-making could lead to concerns about AI's "black box" nature and undermine trust in AI systems.

Public Perception and Cultural Factors: Public perception of AI, shaped by media portrayals and cultural narratives, could impact AI adoption. Negative portrayals or sensationalized stories about AI's potential dangers might foster resistance to AI technologies.

Technological Singularity Concerns: The concept of technological singularity, where AI becomes superintelligent and surpasses human intelligence, raises existential risks. Fear of losing control over AI and its consequences might lead to caution or restrictions in AI development.

Navigating the potential fall of AI requires a balanced approach that addresses technical, ethical, and societal concerns. Collaboration between AI developers, policymakers, researchers, and the public is crucial to building trustworthy and responsible AI systems that benefit humanity and align with societal values. By acknowledging and addressing challenges proactively, we can strive to ensure that AI's journey continues on a trajectory that is ethical, sustainable, and beneficial for all.

Tensions Between Human and AI Forces

The tensions between human and AI forces represent the complex and evolving relationship between artificial intelligence and human society. As AI technologies continue to advance, they interact with various aspects of human life, raising both opportunities and challenges. Here are some key aspects to consider regarding the tensions between human and AI forces:

Economic Disruptions: AI-driven automation can lead to job displacements and changes in the labor market. While AI can enhance productivity and efficiency, it also raises concerns about potential economic inequality and the need for workforce reskilling and adaptation.

Ethical Dilemmas: AI's decision-making and actions can raise ethical dilemmas, especially when it comes to issues of fairness, transparency, accountability, and privacy. Ensuring that AI aligns with human values and adheres to ethical standards is a critical challenge.

Loss of Human Skills: As AI systems become more capable, there is a concern that certain human skills might erode. Overreliance on AI for tasks traditionally performed by humans could lead to a decline in human competencies and autonomy.

Human-AI Collaboration: The relationship between humans and AI can involve both collaboration and competition. Effective human-AI collaboration can augment human capabilities and decision-making. However, striking the right balance to ensure that humans remain in control and that AI is a useful tool is crucial.

Trust and Explainability: Building trust in AI systems is essential for their widespread acceptance and adoption. AI's decisions must be explainable and interpretable to enable users to understand how AI arrives at its conclusions, especially in critical applications like healthcare and autonomous vehicles.

Fear of Job Displacement: The fear of AI-driven job displacement can lead to skepticism and resistance to AI technologies. Ensuring that AI complements human skills rather than replacing them entirely is vital for minimizing these fears.

Security and Privacy Concerns: AI can pose security and privacy risks, such as AI-generated deepfake content or AI-enhanced cyberattacks. Addressing these concerns is necessary to protect individuals and organizations from potential harm.

Autonomy and Human Oversight: As AI becomes more autonomous, the question of how much control humans should retain over AI decisions becomes increasingly important. Balancing autonomy with human oversight is essential to avoid undesirable outcomes.

Cultural and Societal Impact: AI's impact on culture and society is multifaceted. It can influence media consumption, social interactions, and cultural norms. Navigating these changes requires ongoing dialogue and examination of AI's societal implications.

Technological Singularity: The concept of technological singularity, where AI becomes superintelligent and surpasses human intelligence, raises existential questions and concerns about humanity's future.

Managing the tensions between human and AI forces requires a collaborative effort from researchers, policymakers, industry leaders, and the public. Ethical AI development, transparency, regulation, and ongoing dialogue are essential to harness the transformative potential of AI while mitigating its risks. By fostering responsible AI practices, societies can shape the future of human-AI interaction in a way that benefits humanity and upholds human values.

Unforeseen Consequences

Unforeseen consequences with AI forces refer to unexpected outcomes or impacts that arise from the deployment and interaction of artificial intelligence technologies in various domains. As AI becomes more prevalent in society, it can lead to unintended and sometimes undesirable consequences. Here are some key aspects to consider regarding unforeseen consequences with AI forces:

Bias and Discrimination: AI algorithms can perpetuate biases present in the data they are trained on, leading to discriminatory outcomes. Unintentional biases in AI systems can result in unfair decisions in areas such as hiring, lending, and law enforcement.

AI's Impact on Employment: While AI-driven automation can lead to increased productivity, it can also result in job displacement. The impact on the job market and potential shifts in employment patterns may have far-reaching consequences for the workforce.

Manipulation of AI Systems: AI systems can be susceptible to manipulation and adversarial attacks, where malicious actors exploit vulnerabilities to deceive AI algorithms and influence their decisions.

Ethical Dilemmas in Decision-Making: AI's decision-making capabilities raise ethical dilemmas, especially in critical areas like healthcare and autonomous vehicles. The "Trolley Problem" is an example where AI may need to make difficult ethical decisions with no clear "right" answer.

Amplification of Misinformation: AI algorithms on social media platforms can inadvertently amplify the spread of misinformation and fake news, contributing to the polarization of public discourse.

Privacy and Surveillance Concerns: The widespread use of AI in surveillance and facial recognition technologies raises concerns about privacy violations and the potential for mass surveillance without consent.

Unintended Learning and Adaptation: AI systems can learn from unanticipated data sources, leading to unexpected behaviors or results. This unintentional learning could introduce biases or generate inappropriate content.

Dependency on AI: As AI systems become more integrated into various aspects of life, there may be a growing dependence on AI, potentially reducing human agency and decision-making.

AI's Impact on Creativity and Innovation: AI-generated content, such as music, art, and writing, raises questions about the originality and authenticity of creative works, potentially impacting human creativity and innovation.

AI's Environmental Footprint: The extensive computational resources required to train and run AI models have significant environmental implications, contributing to increased energy consumption and carbon emissions.

Addressing unforeseen consequences with AI forces requires proactive measures and ongoing research. Developers and policymakers must prioritize AI safety, transparency, and ethical considerations. Collaborative efforts involving experts from diverse fields can help anticipate potential risks and design AI systems that align with societal values while minimizing unintended negative impacts. Responsible and accountable AI practices are essential to ensuring that AI technologies contribute positively to human progress and well-being.

Chapter 11: Lessons Learned

The journey of artificial intelligence (AI) has been filled with both successes and challenges, offering valuable lessons that shape its future development and integration into society. "Lessons Learned" delves into the key takeaways from the evolution of AI, highlighting the importance of responsible AI development and ethical considerations. Here are some essential lessons learned from the AI journey:

Ethical AI Development: One of the most significant lessons is the critical importance of ethical AI development. AI systems must be designed with a focus on fairness, transparency, accountability, and privacy to ensure they align with human values and avoid unintended consequences.

Addressing Bias and Discrimination: AI algorithms can inherit biases present in the data they are trained on. Recognizing and addressing bias is crucial to avoid perpetuating discriminatory practices and to create AI systems that are fair and inclusive.

Human-Centric AI Design: Putting humans at the center of AI design is essential. AI should complement human capabilities, enhance decision-making, and empower individuals, rather than replacing human roles entirely.

Explainability and Interpretability: AI algorithms should be explainable and interpretable, enabling users to understand how AI arrives at its decisions. This transparency is critical for building trust and accountability in AI systems.

Collaboration between AI and Humans: Fostering effective collaboration between AI and humans is vital. AI should be designed to work alongside humans, enabling synergistic relationships that leverage AI's strengths while incorporating human oversight and guidance.

The Power of Data: Data is the lifeblood of AI, and access to quality, diverse, and unbiased data is crucial for building robust and accurate AI models. Ethical data collection and data privacy measures must be upheld throughout AI development.

Learning from Mistakes: AI researchers and developers must learn from past mistakes and failures to continually improve AI technologies. Adopting a culture of learning and iterating on AI systems can drive progress and innovation.

Responsible Deployment: The responsible deployment of AI technologies requires considering potential risks and societal impacts. Adequate regulations and guidelines are necessary to ensure AI systems operate safely and ethically.

Human Oversight and Decision-Making: While AI can automate tasks and decision-making, maintaining human oversight and control is essential, particularly in areas with significant consequences, such as healthcare, legal, and military domains.

Collaboration and Interdisciplinarity: The complexity of AI challenges necessitates collaboration among experts from diverse disciplines, including AI researchers, ethicists, policymakers, psychologists, and domain specialists.

Continuous Adaptation and Flexibility: AI technologies evolve rapidly, and developers must remain flexible and adaptable to new insights and discoveries. Constantly refining AI systems based on feedback and new research is crucial.

AI for Social Good: AI's potential for positive impact on society should be harnessed to address pressing global challenges, improve healthcare, education, sustainability, and promote inclusivity.

Preparing for the Future: Anticipating future AI developments and their implications allows societies to proactively address ethical, legal, and social challenges before they become significant issues.

Learning from Unforeseen Consequences: Unforeseen consequences with AI forces underscore the need for vigilance and continuous monitoring of AI systems. Learning from these consequences and taking corrective action is essential to refine AI technologies responsibly.

In conclusion, the lessons learned from the journey of AI provide valuable insights into building a future where AI positively contributes to human well-being and societal progress. Responsible AI development, ethical considerations, and human-centric design are foundational principles that guide AI's evolution toward a future that benefits all of humanity. By reflecting on these lessons, we can shape AI technologies to create a more equitable, inclusive, and sustainable world.

In the aftermath of the fall of AI, humanity reflects on the lessons learned and the implications of our journey with artificial intelligence. We examine the importance of responsible AI development and the path towards a symbiotic relationship between humans and machines.

Lessons That Shape AI's Future Development

The lessons that shape AI's future development are crucial takeaways from the past and present advancements in artificial intelligence. These lessons serve as guiding principles to inform the responsible and sustainable development of AI technologies in the future. Here are some key lessons that shape AI's future development:

Ethical and Human-Centric AI: The importance of ethical AI development cannot be overstated. Ensuring that AI technologies are designed with human values and well-being in mind will be crucial in shaping AI's future impact on society. Human-centric AI design should prioritize augmenting human capabilities and decision-making rather than replacing humans.

Transparency and Explainability: Transparency and explainability are essential for building trust and accountability in AI systems. Future AI technologies should be designed to provide understandable explanations for their decisions and actions, enabling users to comprehend and trust AI's behavior.

Addressing Bias and Discrimination: Recognizing and mitigating bias in AI algorithms will be critical in creating fair and inclusive AI systems. Developers must actively work to identify and address biases in AI training data and algorithms to prevent discriminatory outcomes.

Responsible Data Use: AI's reliance on data underscores the importance of responsible data collection, storage, and usage. Future AI development should prioritize data privacy, security, and ethical data sharing practices.

Human Oversight and Control: While AI can automate tasks and decision-making, maintaining human oversight and control is vital, especially in areas with significant consequences such as healthcare, finance, and security.

Collaborative Research and Regulation: Future AI development should involve collaboration among researchers, policymakers, and industry stakeholders to collectively address challenges and set guidelines for responsible AI deployment.

AI Safety and Security: AI safety research must continue to address potential risks associated with AI technologies, ensuring that they operate safely and robustly, with appropriate fail-safe mechanisms.

Preparing for Unforeseen Consequences: AI's rapid evolution requires vigilance and proactive measures to address unforeseen consequences. Constant monitoring and learning from AI applications will help refine and improve future AI technologies responsibly.

Education and AI Literacy: Promoting AI literacy and education will be crucial in shaping the future of AI. Ensuring that individuals understand AI's capabilities, limitations, and ethical implications will foster informed decision-making and responsible AI use.

AI for Social Good: Emphasizing the use of AI for social good will be essential in driving AI's positive impact on society. Encouraging AI applications that address societal challenges, improve healthcare, and promote sustainability will shape AI's future in a positive direction.

Long-Term Considerations: Future AI development must consider long-term implications, including potential societal shifts, economic impacts, and environmental considerations.

Regulatory Frameworks: Developing effective regulatory frameworks will be essential in guiding AI development and ensuring compliance with ethical and legal standards.

AI Collaboration and Interoperability: Enabling interoperability and collaboration between different AI systems will facilitate AI's potential for addressing complex challenges that require multi-disciplinary solutions.

Continuous Innovation and Research: AI's future development relies on continuous innovation and research to push the boundaries of what AI can achieve while maintaining ethical and responsible practices.

By applying these lessons to the future development of AI, researchers, policymakers, and stakeholders can collectively shape AI technologies that positively contribute to humanity's well-being, foster inclusivity, and address global challenges responsibly. Responsible AI development practices will be instrumental in shaping a future where AI technologies enhance human lives, promote fairness, and support sustainable development.

The Importance of Responsible AI Development

Responsible AI development is of paramount importance as artificial intelligence technologies become increasingly integrated into various aspects of our lives. Responsible AI development refers to the ethical and thoughtful approach to designing, building, and deploying AI systems that prioritize human well-being, fairness, transparency, and accountability. Here are key reasons why responsible AI development is crucial:

Ensuring Ethical Practices: Responsible AI development requires considering the ethical implications of AI technologies. It involves avoiding biases, discrimination, and harm to individuals or communities. Ethical AI is essential to maintain public trust and avoid negative consequences.

Mitigating Bias and Discrimination: AI algorithms can perpetuate biases present in the data they are trained on, leading to discriminatory outcomes. Responsible AI development involves identifying and mitigating bias, promoting fairness and inclusivity.

Fostering Trust and Adoption: Trust is fundamental for the widespread adoption of AI technologies. Responsible AI practices, including transparency, explainability, and human oversight, build trust and confidence in AI systems.

Protecting Privacy and Data Security: AI often relies on vast amounts of data. Responsible AI development ensures that data privacy is respected, and measures are in place to secure sensitive information from unauthorized access or misuse.

Minimizing Unintended Consequences: AI systems can produce unintended outcomes due to their complexity and learning from data. Responsible AI development involves ongoing monitoring and learning from mistakes to avoid undesirable consequences.

Enhancing Human-Centric Design: Responsible AI development focuses on creating AI technologies that augment human capabilities rather than replacing human roles entirely. Human-centric design ensures that AI serves human needs and values.

Promoting Accountability: Responsible AI development incorporates mechanisms for accountability, enabling users and developers to understand and explain AI decisions and actions. This fosters accountability for AI system behavior.

Addressing Global Challenges: AI has the potential to address significant global challenges, such as climate change, healthcare, and education. Responsible AI development ensures that AI is harnessed for social good and sustainable development.

Regulatory Compliance: Responsible AI development aligns with relevant regulations and legal frameworks. It involves staying informed about evolving laws and guidelines related to AI technologies.

Avoiding Concentration of Power: Unchecked AI development may lead to the concentration of power in the hands of a few entities. Responsible AI development promotes fair competition and diverse AI ecosystems.

Safeguarding Against Malicious Use: Responsible AI development involves considering potential security risks and deploying safeguards against malicious uses of AI, such as AI-driven misinformation or cyberattacks.

Long-Term Considerations: Responsible AI development takes into account the long-term impacts of AI technologies, including societal changes, economic consequences, and the potential for unintended consequences over time.

Promoting Global Collaboration: Responsible AI development encourages collaboration among different stakeholders, including researchers, policymakers, industry, and the public, to collectively address AI challenges and opportunities.

In conclusion, responsible AI development is a moral and ethical imperative. It ensures that AI technologies are designed and deployed with the well-being of individuals, society, and the environment in mind. By prioritizing ethics, transparency, fairness, and accountability, we can shape AI's future in a way that maximizes its benefits while minimizing potential risks and negative impacts. Responsible AI development is essential to create a future where AI technologies empower humanity, contribute positively to society, and align with our collective values and aspirations.

Chapter 12: A New Dawn

The final chapter offers a glimpse of the future, post-AI fall, and how humanity rebuilds. We explore the potential for AI's resurrection, the ethical considerations that guide future AI endeavors, and the role of AI in shaping a brighter tomorrow.

"A New Dawn" symbolizes the beginning of a transformative era shaped by the continued evolution of artificial intelligence. This chapter explores the exciting possibilities and challenges that lie ahead as AI technologies progress and become more deeply integrated into society. Here are some key aspects of the new dawn of AI:

AI Augmented Human Intelligence: The new era of AI will focus on augmenting human intelligence rather than replacing it. AI technologies will empower individuals with powerful tools to enhance decision-making, problem-solving, and creativity across various domains.

Personalized AI Experiences: AI will offer increasingly personalized experiences, from personalized learning platforms to AI-driven healthcare tailored to an individual's unique needs. This personalization will lead to more effective and customized services for each individual.

AI for Sustainability: AI's potential for optimizing resource use, monitoring environmental changes, and supporting sustainable practices will play a vital role in addressing global challenges such as climate change, resource conservation, and ecological preservation.

Autonomous Systems and Robotics: The new dawn of AI will witness the proliferation of autonomous systems and robotics in various sectors, including transportation, manufacturing, agriculture, and healthcare, leading to increased efficiency and safety.

AI and Creativity: AI-generated content, including art, music, literature, and design, will inspire new forms of creative expression and collaboration between human creators and AI algorithms.

AI-Driven Healthcare Revolution: AI-powered medical diagnostics, drug discovery, and personalized treatments will revolutionize healthcare, leading to earlier disease detection, more effective therapies, and improved patient outcomes.

Ethical AI Governance: A new era of AI will demand robust and adaptable regulatory frameworks that address the ethical, privacy, and security considerations of AI technologies. Ethical AI governance will be essential in fostering responsible AI development.

Global Collaboration in AI Research: Collaboration among researchers, institutions, and countries will accelerate AI advancements. Open AI research and knowledge sharing will fuel innovation and ensure AI benefits are accessible to all.

AI in Education and Lifelong Learning: AI's integration in education will transform traditional learning models, making education more accessible, engaging, and tailored to individual needs throughout a person's lifelong learning journey.

AI in Space Exploration: AI's potential to analyze vast amounts of data will support space exploration efforts, enabling more sophisticated data processing, spacecraft autonomy, and planetary exploration.

Human-Robot Collaboration: Collaborative environments where humans and robots work together in harmony will become more prevalent, enhancing productivity and safety across various industries.

AI in Disaster Response and Humanitarian Aid: AI technologies will aid in disaster prediction, early warning systems, and efficient disaster response, saving lives and providing timely aid to affected communities.

AI and Social Impact: AI will continue to drive social impact by addressing critical challenges such as poverty, hunger, and public health, fostering sustainable development and equality.

AI Ethical Considerations: As AI becomes more capable, the importance of ethical considerations will grow. Ensuring AI technologies prioritize human values, fairness, and accountability will be crucial in shaping the positive impact of AI.

In conclusion, the new dawn of AI holds tremendous promise for humanity, offering transformative solutions to global challenges and opportunities for human empowerment. To fully embrace this new era, stakeholders must prioritize responsible AI development, ethical considerations, and collaborative efforts to ensure that AI technologies benefit all of humanity. By leveraging AI's potential while addressing its challenges, we can shape a future where AI serves as a catalyst for positive change and paves the way for a more sustainable, inclusive, and enlightened world.

The Ethical Considerations That Guide Future AI

The ethical considerations that guide future AI development play a pivotal role in shaping AI technologies' impact on society. As AI technologies continue to advance, it becomes increasingly important to prioritize ethical principles to ensure responsible, fair, and beneficial deployment. Here are key ethical considerations that should guide the development of AI in the future:

Fairness and Avoiding Bias: AI algorithms must be designed and trained to be fair and unbiased, avoiding discrimination based on factors like race, gender, or other protected attributes. Developers should implement techniques to identify and mitigate bias in data and algorithms.

Transparency and Explainability: AI systems should be transparent and provide understandable explanations for their decisions and actions. Ensuring that AI operates in an interpretable manner enhances user trust and allows for human oversight.

Privacy and Data Protection: Respect for user privacy is essential in AI development. Systems must adhere to data protection regulations and use personal data responsibly, with explicit consent and robust security measures.

Accountability and Responsibility: Developers, organizations, and users of AI systems should be accountable for the technology's outcomes. Establishing clear lines of responsibility helps ensure that potential harms are addressed appropriately.

Human Autonomy and Control: Human autonomy should be preserved, and AI systems should be designed to support human decision-making, not replace it entirely. Humans should retain control over critical decisions and have the ability to override AI suggestions.

Avoiding Malevolent Use: Developers must consider potential malevolent uses of AI and design systems with safeguards to prevent misuse or exploitation of AI technologies for harmful purposes.

Social Impact and Inclusivity: AI development should prioritize social impact and inclusivity, ensuring that AI technologies benefit all members of society and do not exacerbate existing inequalities.

Sustainable and Ethical Business Models: Organizations developing AI should prioritize sustainable and ethical business practices, avoiding exploitative or unethical uses of AI technologies.

Informed Consent and User Empowerment: Users interacting with AI systems should be informed about how their data is used and have the ability to make informed decisions about AI-enabled services and features.

Avoiding Dehumanization: AI technologies should be designed to avoid dehumanization, respecting human dignity and ensuring that AI is used to enhance human capabilities and well-being.

Long-Term Consequences: Consideration of the long-term consequences of AI technologies is essential. Developers should anticipate and address potential future challenges or societal impacts.

Global Collaboration and Knowledge Sharing: Collaboration among researchers, policymakers, and stakeholders on a global scale is crucial for setting international standards and guidelines for ethical AI development.

Ethical AI Governance: Establishing robust ethical AI governance frameworks, including ethical review boards and mechanisms for ongoing monitoring and oversight, will promote responsible AI development.

AI for Social Good: Prioritizing the use of AI technologies for social good, such as addressing global challenges and improving public services, can maximize AI's positive impact on society.

By adhering to these ethical considerations, the future development and deployment of AI technologies can be shaped in a way that benefits humanity, fosters trust, and ensures AI's responsible integration into various aspects of life. Ethical AI development is an ongoing process, requiring continuous reflection, adaptability, and collaboration to create a future where AI serves as a force for positive change and collective well-being.

The Role of AI In Shaping a Brighter Tomorrow

Artificial intelligence (AI) plays a transformative role in shaping a brighter and more promising future for humanity across various domains. As AI technologies continue to evolve, they offer immense potential to address global challenges, empower individuals, and promote sustainable development. Here are some key ways in which AI can contribute to a brighter tomorrow:

Advancing Healthcare: AI-driven medical diagnostics, personalized treatments, and drug discovery can revolutionize healthcare, leading to earlier disease detection, improved patient outcomes, and more effective healthcare delivery.

Enhancing Education: AI-powered educational tools and personalized learning platforms can revolutionize the education landscape, making learning more accessible, engaging, and tailored to individual needs.

Fostering Sustainability: AI can optimize resource usage, monitor environmental changes, and enable smart cities, contributing to more sustainable practices and mitigating the impact of climate change.

Improving Agricultural Practices: AI technologies can enhance agricultural productivity by providing precision farming techniques, pest detection, and crop management strategies, leading to increased food production and reduced waste.

Enhancing Transportation: AI can improve transportation efficiency, safety, and reduce traffic congestion through autonomous vehicles, smart traffic management, and predictive maintenance of transportation infrastructure.

Enabling Personalized Experiences: AI can offer personalized experiences across various sectors, from e-commerce to entertainment, providing tailored recommendations and services that meet individual preferences.

Assisting in Scientific Discoveries: AI's data processing capabilities can accelerate scientific research and discovery, leading to breakthroughs in fields such as astronomy, climate science, and drug development.

Supporting Disaster Response: AI-driven early warning systems, natural language processing for emergency communication, and autonomous robots for search and rescue can improve disaster response and aid humanitarian efforts.

Promoting Inclusivity: AI can address societal challenges, such as promoting financial inclusion, providing better access to healthcare and education in remote areas, and assisting individuals with disabilities.

Empowering Creative Industries: AI-generated content, such as music, art, and literature, can inspire new forms of creativity, enriching the cultural landscape and encouraging collaboration between humans and AI algorithms.

Revolutionizing Customer Service: AI-powered chatbots and virtual assistants can enhance customer service experiences by providing quick and personalized support to users.

Optimizing Business Operations: AI's ability to analyze large datasets can lead to more efficient business operations, better supply chain management, and improved decision-making.

Driving Scientific Exploration: AI can analyze vast amounts of data from space missions and telescopes, facilitating scientific exploration and unlocking the mysteries of the universe.

Advancing Ethical Considerations: By prioritizing ethical AI development, society can ensure AI's positive impact while mitigating potential risks and challenges.

It is essential to approach AI development responsibly, ensuring that AI technologies align with human values, adhere to ethical standards, and prioritize fairness and transparency. Collaboration between researchers, policymakers, industry leaders, and the public will be critical to address the challenges and opportunities that AI presents. By harnessing the transformative power of AI for the collective good, we can shape a brighter tomorrow where AI technologies work in harmony with humanity, fostering innovation, sustainable development, and well-being for all.

The Epilogue: Embracing a Human-Centric AI Future

As the journey of artificial intelligence unfolds, the epilogue marks a reflection on the past and a vision for the future. The epilogue emphasizes the importance of a human-centric approach to AI, where technological advancements are harnessed to empower and enrich human lives. It calls for a collective commitment to responsible AI development and ethical considerations to shape a future where AI technologies contribute positively to society. Here are some key elements of the epilogue:

A Shared Responsibility: The future of AI is a shared responsibility among researchers, policymakers, industry leaders, and society at large. Collaborative efforts are essential to ensure that AI technologies are designed and deployed in a manner that benefits humanity as a whole.

Ethical AI Governance: Establishing robust ethical AI governance frameworks becomes even more critical as AI technologies advance. Ethical review boards, guidelines, and continuous monitoring mechanisms will guide AI development responsibly.

Balancing Innovation and Ethical Considerations: Striking a balance between innovation and ethical considerations is crucial. The pursuit of technological advancement should always be accompanied by thoughtful reflections on the potential impacts of AI on individuals and society.

Empowering Human Potential: The true essence of AI lies in empowering human potential. AI technologies should augment human capabilities, allowing individuals to focus on creativity, critical thinking, and compassion.

Inclusivity and Equality: Embracing AI for social good involves ensuring inclusivity and equality. AI should not perpetuate existing inequalities but instead strive to bridge the gap and create a more equitable society.

Addressing Unforeseen Challenges: The future of AI is marked by continuous learning and adaptation. Addressing unforeseen challenges and unintended consequences requires flexibility and a commitment to ongoing improvement.

Nurturing AI Literacy: Increasing AI literacy is essential for a better-informed society. Understanding AI's capabilities and limitations will enable individuals to make informed decisions and participate actively in shaping AI's future.

AI and Human Collaboration: The future of AI is not about humans versus machines; it's about human-machine collaboration. AI technologies should amplify human intelligence and foster harmonious interactions.

Fostering a Culture of Responsible AI: Creating a culture of responsible AI development involves valuing ethics, transparency, fairness, and accountability as fundamental principles of AI design and deployment.

A World of Possibilities: The epilogue envisions a world where AI-driven advancements lead to unprecedented possibilities. From addressing global challenges to fostering innovation, AI becomes an integral part of a brighter and more hopeful future.

In conclusion, the epilogue signifies a call to action for embracing a human-centric AI future. It recognizes the potential of AI to revolutionize industries, solve pressing problems, and enhance human experiences. Yet, it emphasizes the importance of responsible AI development, placing humanity's values and well-being at the forefront. By steering AI development with an ethical compass and collective responsibility, we can shape a future where AI technologies are a force for good, fostering a harmonious coexistence between humans and machines, and unleashing the potential for a more inclusive, sustainable, and enlightened world. The epilogue marks not an end but a new beginning in the journey of AI, guided by the vision of a brighter and more promising tomorrow.

In the epilogue, we reflect on the journey of AI, the impact it had on society, and the enduring legacy it leaves behind. The Rise and Fall of Artificial Intelligence serves as a cautionary tale and an inspiration for the future, reminding us of the delicate balance between human ambition and technological progress.

www.ingramcontent.com/pod-product-compliance
Lightning Source LLC
La Vergne TN
LVHW041217050326
832903LV00021B/666